WITHDRAWN

D0603876

RIVERSIDE PUBLIC LIBRARY —

THE
GREATEST
PITCHERS
OF
ALL
TIME

THE GREATEST PITCHERS OF ALL TIME

DONALD HONIG

CROWN PUBLISHERS, INC.
NEW YORK

For my daughter, Catherine

ACKNOWLEDGMENTS

The author would like to express his appreciation to the following for advice and encouragement extended during the writing of this book: Michael P. Aronstein, Stanley Honig, David Markson, Lawrence Ritter, Thomas Brookman, Louis Kiefer, Douglas Mulcahy, and Jeffrey Neuman. Also, a particular expression of gratitude is due William Deane, senior research associate at the National Baseball Hall of Fame and Museum.

Copyright © 1988 by Donald Honig

All rights reserved. No part of this book may be reproduced or transmitted in any form or by any means, electronic or mechanical, including photocopying, recording, or by any information storage and retrieval system, without permission in writing from the publisher.

Published by Crown Publishers, Inc., 225 Park Avenue South, New York, New York 10003, and represented in Canada by the Canadian MANDA Group

CROWN is a trademark of Crown Publishers, Inc.

Manufactured in the United States of America

Library of Congress Cataloging-in-Publication Data
Honig, Donald.
The greatest pitchers of all time.

1. Pitchers (Baseball)—United States—Biography.
I. Title.
GV865.A1H6175   1988   796.357'092'2 [B]
                 87-32960
          ISBN 0-517-56887-X

10 9 8 7 6 5 4 3 2 1

First Edition

Design: Robert Aulicino

By Donald Honig

Nonfiction

Baseball When the Grass Was Real
Baseball Between the Lines
The Man in the Dugout
The October Heroes
The Image of Their Greatness (with Lawrence Ritter)
The 100 Greatest Baseball Players of All Time (with Lawrence Ritter)
The Brooklyn Dodgers: An Illustrated Tribute
The New York Yankees: An Illustrated History
Baseball's 10 Greatest Teams
The Los Angeles Dodgers: The First Quarter Century
The National League: An Illustrated History
The American League: An Illustrated History
The Boston Red Sox: An Illustrated Tribute
Baseball America
The New York Mets: The First Quarter Century
The World Series: An Illustrated History
Baseball in the '50s
The All-Star Game: An Illustrated History
Mays, Mantle, Snider: A Celebration
Baseball's Greatest First Basemen
Baseball's Greatest Pitchers

Fiction

Sidewalk Caesar
Walk Like a Man
The Americans
Divide the Night
No Song to Sing
Judgment Night
The Love Thief
The Severith Style
Illusions
I Should Have Sold Petunias
The Last Great Season
Marching Home

CONTENTS

INTRODUCTION

According to Tom Seaver, "No other sport has such a vivid and dramatic confrontation" as baseball's between pitcher and batter.

In baseball it all begins with the pitcher; nothing happens until he has completed his brief, ceremonial-like windup and has delivered the ball.

One of baseball's unchallenged estimates is that pitching is at least 85 percent of the game. This makes the man who stands atop the small mound in the middle of the diamond the game's most crucial factor. Baseball has gone through many modifications in this century, but the importance of pitching has remained fixed. Teams blessed with strong mound staffs have always been either winners or top contenders, while most clubs that tried to sustain themselves by bat weight alone have finished far off the mark.

Thousands and thousands of men have taken the big-league mounds in this century. Among them have been stars, dependables, journeymen, and mediocrities. And a handful of masters. It is this last group that this book, risking the fires of controversy, chooses to focus on. Selecting the rather arbitrary number of 22 pitchers and holding them up as the greatest of their profession across nearly a full century's scope necessitated omitting many other front-rank performers (some of whom are discussed briefly in the epilogue).

Once upon a time, in the early years of this century, a club carried five or six pitchers, and the starter was expected to complete his game. (They were known as "slab men" or "box men" back then.) Today a club averages 10 pitchers on its roster, and if a starter delivers seven good innings the manager is pleased. Today there are starters, middle-inning relief men, and that much-valued commodity known as "the stopper" or "finisher," who comes on the scene when the fires are at their hottest.

But no matter who he is, no matter when he is out there—at the beginning, in the middle, or at the end—nothing can happen until the pitcher strides forward, whips around his arm, and fires the ball.

Cy Young with Cleveland in 1911, his last year in the big leagues

CY YOUNG

He looms as sort of a patriarch to the pitching fraternity, almost biblical in the begetting of records that read like the spinnings of a fabulist, straining credulity and seeming to cry out for acts of faith. But he was real enough.

He labored in an age of workhorse pitching, when relief pitching was virtually unheard of. While the records of Young's first decade in the major leagues, the 1890s, have a mighty impact on the printed page, they must be read in context. For instance, Young won 36 games for Cleveland in 1892 but didn't lead the league in that department. In 1893 he won 32, and that was the league's third-best total. When he led with 35 wins in 1895, he was one of four 30-game winners in the league. A year later he won 29 and was tied for second in victories.

If in the 1890s Amos Rusie struck out far more batters than Cy did, and Kid Nichols was a more consistent winner, why is baseball's most prestigious pitching award named after Cy Young? The reason is this: While others may have been his equal, it was only temporarily, for no one was as indefatigably excellent for so many years. It was a combination of his brilliant pitching and his durability that have let flow the golden light of legend upon Cy Young.

He must have been one of the most spectacular physical specimens ever to take the mound. He came to the big leagues with Cleveland in 1890, went to St. Louis in 1899, Boston in 1901, back to Cleveland in 1909, and finished with Boston in 1911, at the age of forty-four. That's 22 big-league seasons, and in 16 of them he pitched over 300 innings, in five of them he won over 30 games, and in 16 of them (14 in succession) he won over 20 games. He claimed never to have had a sore arm, which is just as well, for in those days teams carried just a handful of pitchers, and if your arm was sore you just kept working until either the problem went away or you had done irreparable damage to yourself.

Young pitched long enough to be at the top of the list in both wins (511) and losses

(313). The frequency with which he took the mound explains his loss total, but not necessarily that remarkable number of victories. We have seen most of baseball's once-inviolable tablets smashed—Babe Ruth's lifetime and single-season home-run records, Ty Cobb's all-time hit and stolen-base totals, Walter Johnson's lifetime strikeout total; but it is highly unlikely that we will ever see anyone even approach Young's 511 wins.

He was Denton True Young at birth, which took place in Gilmore, Ohio, on March 29, 1867. He died on November 4, 1955, at the age of eighty-eight, a handsome span of time, and most appropriate for one of baseball's longevity wonders. (A year after his death the Cy Young Memorial Award for annual pitching excellence was created.)

When Cy began his career, the pitcher stood on a flat piece of ground 50 feet from the batter, caught by a catcher who wore on his hand nothing more than an ordinary men's dress glove. When he retired (after having been the only pitcher to star throughout the 1890s and the entire first decade of the new century), the pitcher stood 60 feet, 6 inches away, working off a mound that was topped with a slab of hard rubber, and the catcher wore enough equipment to look like a knight of the Crusades.

Young Denton grew up on his father's farm, developing that hearty physique doing the usual chores, including splitting rails, which he claimed helped immensely. "Swinging an ax," he said, "hardens the hands and builds up the shoulders and back." The Nautilus equipment of yore.

He was doing some pitching around Ohio's hill country when he received an offer from the Canton club in the Tri-State

Cy Young in 1908

League. This was in 1890. The story is that he threw so hard that a sportswriter nicknamed him "Cyclone"; the name stuck and was inevitably shortened to Cy.

After splitting 30 decisions at Canton, Cy was sold to Cleveland, then in the National League. The price was reportedly $250. He finished the 1890 season with a 9–7 record. The next year he won 27, and it would be 1905 before he failed to win at least 20 in a season.

Young remained with Cleveland until 1898, when the club owner purchased the St. Louis franchise and brought along his stars with him, including Young. Cy pitched in St. Louis for two years, but he cared neither for the city nor for its blazing-hot summers. So when Ban Johnson formed the American League in 1901 and offered Cy a salary of $3,000 to jump, the great pitcher was receptive. (The National League, enjoying its monopoly status, had a $2,400 salary ceiling, take it or leave it. These were the acorns that would one day grow into the great oaks of the Major League Players Association and free agency.)

Cy signed on with the brand-new Boston American League club, then known as the Pilgrims. He was then thirty-three years old and big-bellied, and the National League, chagrined at losing one of its star performers to the upstart league, chewed on some sour grapes and said the portly pitcher was over the hill.

Well, if Cy was over the hill, he quickly found another one, a better one. For his first three American League seasons he was 33–10, 32–10, and 28–10.

In 1903 Boston won the pennant and participated in the first World Series ever played, against the Pittsburgh Pirates. The Series was an opportunity for the fledgling American League to establish parity with the older National League, who still regarded the newcomers with disdain. Cy and his Boston teammates shattered once and for all the National League's illusion of superiority by winning the best-of-nine competition in eight games, with Young winning twice.

The following year, on May 5, Cy turned in his greatest single effort, a perfect game against the Philadelphia Athletics. It was his second no-hitter, the first coming on September 18, 1897, against Cincinnati. He coughed up a then-record third no-hitter against New York on June 30, 1908.

After the 1908 season, Cy was sold to Cleveland for $12,500, a pretty fancy price tag in those days. Forty-two years old now, fronted by a big, round belly, he was 19–15 in 1909, his last productive year.

Cleveland released the living legend in August 1911, and he signed with the Boston Braves, with whom he ended his major-league career with a 4–5 record.

The old boy retired to his Ohio farm to contemplate his remarkable career. He lived on and on, through a world war, a depression, another world war, a war in Korea, getting older and older, his glory years remoter, his records more improbable. And all the while fans and writers made endless journeys of devotion to sit and talk of names and games and days long gone into the swirling eddies of time. How, they wanted to know, could a man win 511 big-league games, far more than Walter Johnson, Christy Mathewson, or Grover Cleveland Alexander, who had become generally acclaimed as the three greatest pitchers of all time?

"Never had a sore arm," Cy would tell them. "Even though I usually pitched

Cy *(right)* with his favorite catcher, Lou Criger

with just two days' rest and sometimes just one. Oh, it would get tired sometimes, but that never bothered me." In fact, the old man would tell them, it wasn't a worn-out arm that finally retired him, but that big belly. "I had trouble fielding bunts, you see," he said. "The boys saw that and they just kept dropping 'em down on me. Was nothing wrong with my arm."

And what did this grand old monument deliver up to the plate?

"A couple of good curve balls," he said. "One was an overhand pitch that broke sharply down, the other a sidearm sweeper. I'd wheel on the batter so as to hide the pitch, and I had excellent control. And I had that fast ball too. It was plenty fast. A whistler. Listen, I saw Amos Rusie, Walter Johnson, Lefty Grove, Bob Feller. They were the fast ones. But I was right with them."

Well, an old man might tell some tales. But when he has won 511 games, you listen.

The 511-game winner loosening up

Rube Waddell: "He loved parties, booze, pretty women, red neckties, and ice cream by the quart. . . ."

RUBE WADDELL

Rube Waddell, the greatest left-handed pitcher of his day, and maybe of anybody's day, evoked descriptive words wherever he went. He was, they said, eccentric, gregarious, lovable, uninhibited, childlike, unpredictable. If left-handers are truly baseball's oddballs, as tradition has it, then their patron saint is Rube Waddell.

Connie Mack's fast-balling turn-of-the-century left-hander has left behind his own unique anecdotes. For instance, it is claimed that Rube once wrestled an alligator in Florida. It is said that the sound of a fire engine would bring him running, even out of a ball park in full uniform, and, if he could, jumping onto the horse-drawn vehicle. (Connie said, years later, "I was always afraid he'd fall off one of those engines and hurt his arm." Notice, not his head or his leg or his neck. Even the saintly Connie had his priorities.) And it is a fact that a playful bit of roughhousing with a teammate cost him an injured shoulder and a chance to pitch in the 1905 World Series.

Waddell loved parties and booze and pretty women and red neckties and ice cream by the quart, and as long as his fast ball sizzled like static electricity he had as much of them as he wanted. Most of all he loved to go fishing, and Connie would say, "Rube, win this one and you can take a couple of days off and try your luck in the streams," whereupon Rube would surely win it and then go off for those few days like some unreconstructed Huck Finn, his big, foolish heart filled with delight.

Connie indulged him, and the world fussed over him and bought him drinks and slapped that big back and those broad shoulders and made Rube the center of attention wherever he went. And it was all predicated not upon wit or wealth or power but rather upon a fast ball that Rube could discharge, they said, as fast as any man alive. He called it his "thunderball," and he matched it with a curve that today sounds as if it broke from Maine to the Baja Peninsula. Yes, the big fellow could pitch.

7

George Edward Waddell arrived on the planet Earth from somewhere else on October 13, 1876, at Bradford, Pennsylvania. A contemporary had this description of him: "Full of fun and laughter, very good-natured." This brief portrait dated from the time Rube was about nine years old; it would never have to be revised or updated.

He grew into a strapping young man, an inch or two over six feet, just under 200 pounds. Somewhere along the line, somebody put a baseball in his left hand, and destiny began whirling its cylinders. Rube was pitching for a semipro team in Franklin, Pennsylvania, in 1897, when he got an offer from Fred Clarke, manager of the Louisville club to come down to Kentucky to pitch. No mere offer, this— Louisville was at that time in the National League.

So the twenty-year-old Rube vaulted from semipro to big leaguer. But not for long. After appearing in just two games he went off on a toot, and when Clarke fined him $50 for the adventure, an indignant Waddell jumped the club. Rube, operating under unassailable logic, said later, "The team is supposed to give you money, not take it away."

Over the next few years Waddell pitched for various clubs, including Grand Rapids (Michigan) in the Western League, where one of his opponents was Sam Crawford, later to become one of baseball's most princely big boppers. In a conversation with writer Lawrence Ritter years later, Crawford recalled the young Rube Waddell:

> You had to notice him. First, because he was such a big kid. Then, because of that fast ball. And once you started noticing him, you found you never took your eyes off of him. He

was always laughing out there on the mound. That's because the other side tried to keep him in good humor, even when he was striking them all out. They figured he was tough enough to hit against when he was happy; get him mad and there was no telling.

Rube was back with Louisville in 1899—Fred Clarke could not resist the allure of that fast ball—posting a 7–2 record. In 1900 the club moved to Pittsburgh, and "the big happy-go-lucky slob" (Clarke's tender description) rang up a 9–11 record but led the league in strikeouts with 133. Clarke, however, ran out of patience with his zany left-hander and dealt him to the Cubs early in 1901. Rube lasted one year in Chicago, going 13–16.

George Edward (Rube) Waddell

A year later he turned up with Connie Mack's Philadelphia Athletics.

Connie was known as a rather stern disciplinarian. He preferred his players to be well-behaved, well-dressed when on the road, and sober. He pioneered in enticing college-bred players into major-league ball, striving to make the game—then known for rowdyism—more socially acceptable. This was commendable and all to the good, but Connie was also an incorrigible baseball junkie, and when he saw the untamable Rube and his un-hittable smoker, the skipper put first things first.

So Connie bent a bit in the high winds of Rube's private carnival and allowed him his peccadilloes. Connie was always praised by one and all as a handler of men, and he was never more deft than

Rube during his heyday years with the Athletics

with Rube (and never mind some grumbling from the other players about favoritism). Rube could go fishing, he could take an afternoon off and sit in a firehouse indulging his peculiar fascination—as long as he delivered on the mound.

And deliver he did. From 1902 through 1905 his win totals were 23, 21, 25, and 26. He led in strikeouts in each of those years as well as the next two. In 1903 he whiffed 301, which was 126 more than the runner-up, a telltale indication of how hard Waddell threw. In 1904 he established a league record with 349 strikeouts—this in an era of chokeup, contact hitters. He must really have raised blisters on the air of those mellow long-ago summers. That record stood for 69 years, until Nolan Ryan broke it in 1973.

Connie Mack

He was the toast of Philadelphia, and he loved every moment of it. When Rube laughed, everybody laughed, and when Rube drank, everybody drank. "The minute he stepped into a saloon," one old-timer writer recalled, "everything became jovial. Sometimes he'd shuck his coat and go behind the bar and serve as bartender. Everybody loved him." Yes, they surely did. He was the town's premier attraction, along with the Liberty Bell, also slightly cracked.

But fast living and fast balls don't go together for very long. During the 1907 season Connie saw that Rube's "thunderball" was starting to lose some of its hurry, and even though the big lefty was still a winner (19–13), his talents were no longer outweighing the sleepless nights he caused. The AWOL fishing trips weren't being followed by a buzz of automatic, expiating victories. Connie dealt him to St. Louis.

Rube had a decent 1908 for the Browns—19–14—and then slipped to 11–14 the following year. The supply of fast balls was thinning now, and with them the adoring backslappers.

There must have been a bit of confusion in Rube's quaint and uncomplicated mind now. This heartily gregarious fellow always thought they loved him for himself, and no doubt some did; but that fast ball had been the raison d'être for his celebrity, almost the basis of his very existence, and when it went so did the applause and the noisy adulators. Now there were gaps in the crowd and snickers in the laughter. By 1910 Rube was out of the big leagues.

He hung on, doing the only thing he knew, in his innocence probably believing it would all come back to him. He pitched for Newark, for Minneapolis, then

Rube with the St. Louis Browns in 1909

sank to the lower minors, where the bushers dug in on him and took solid potshots at the best he had, and Rube no doubt wondered where it had all gone, why his left arm had betrayed him. But of course the big guy had been dancing on eggshells all along.

But soon his vanished fast ball was the least of his problems, for Rube was now in his final, fatal spin.

In the spring of 1913 he had been living in the town of Hickman, Kentucky. Heavy rains and melting snows caused the waters to come rushing down the mountains and roaring through the levee. Among hundreds of volunteers stacking bags of sand was George Edward Waddell. The soaking he received from standing in the icy waters penetrated to his very marrow, and soon he was wracked with tuberculosis, in those years a sure death sentence.

With the help of a friend, he entered a sanitorium in San Antonio. The handwriting was on the scoreboard now. Rube's once robust frame shrank and withered to 110 pounds as he lay waiting to die, entertaining Lord only knows what thoughts and memories.

The life that he had taken so merrily and naively for granted continued to seep out of him until the bucket emptied. The date was April 1, 1914. April Fool's Day. Make of it what you will.

Matty getting loose. Note that glove.

CHRISTY MATHEWSON

Baseball has been taken not only into the heart of America but also into its sweetest dreams and most cherished fantasies. Nothing, not war or depression or scandal, has ever been able to impinge on its growth or well-being. And when one of those scandals did become a bit ominous (after the revelations of the 1919 World Series fix), the game suddenly received a cyclonic rejuvenation named Babe Ruth. In fact, so blessed is this bloodstream American game that once upon a time, when it was considered by many as a profession for rowdies and drunkards, it saw the timely entry into its ranks of one of the most lordly specimens of young manhood ever to enlighten the sporting scene.

It has been written that if Babe Ruth had not been born it would have been impossible to invent him. Well, while Christy Mathewson might not have been so taxing a challenge to the imagination, it might have been difficult to make him believable. He was tall, strong, nobly handsome; he was intelligent and schol- arly; he was a superb athlete able to star at both football and baseball; he was the successful suitor of his college sweetheart, with whom he enjoyed a long and happy marriage. Take all this and inject just enough Tabasco into the persona to make the virtues seem nobler than they already are, then allow it to chill awhile, just enough to leave a cool, slightly offputting aura, and you have the mystique of Christy Mathewson, his generation's "greatest pitcher that ever lived."

He was the first American sports hero whose appeal crossed all social, economic, and cultural boundaries. The fans worshiped him, the press idealized him, his teammates revered him. To many people, he made baseball a "respectable" profession, and he did it not by preaching or by trying to set an example, but simply by being himself, a figure simultaneously awesome and inspiring, who never lost that touch of the aristocratic, the aloof, which seemed so naturally a part of him.

"He never tried to be different," Giants teammate Rube Marquard said years later. "He never thought he was better than anybody else. It was just the way he carried himself. It was the way we saw him. But it was okay, because, what the hell, when you come down to it, he *was* different, and on that mound he *was* better than anybody else."

One writer described him this way: "He makes you think of a good-looking boy who has grown up to be a man without becoming commonplace." Christy's eyes "kind of smile and sparkle and glow in harmony with the drift of his conversation." The Mathewson voice was "low, full, and rather melodious. . . . it rolls out easily, but just a trifle slow. There is a note of honest clearness in the tone that makes a man feel comfortable." The writer wound up this 1909 depiction thus: "Mathewson talks like a Harvard graduate, looks like an actor, acts like a business man, and impresses you as an all-round gentleman."

He was born in Factoryville, Pennsylvania, on August 12, 1880. This small northeastern Pennsylvania town was, according to its most famous son, a place "where they used to pull down the shades on Sunday. There was an atmosphere of calm and quiet on the first day of the week and an almost religious tinge in the air. I had been brought up rather strictly among sober country folks who considered the evils of drink a national calamity, and criticized many things to which New York would never give a second thought."

His mother wanted him to be a preacher, but "I never gave the matter serious thought," Christy said. "Certainly as far back as that age when every boy contrasts the advantages of being a pirate or

Christy Mathewson in 1906

an Indian hunter, and tries to determine in which particular profession he would be most likely to shine, I chose the profession of a baseball player." In other words, all the impulses of a future 373-game winner were vibrating at an early age.

He began pitching in earnest when he was attending a local school, the Keystone Academy. He took to pitching, he said, "naturally enough."

From the Keystone Academy, Mathewson went on to Bucknell College, where he became one of the most prominent men on campus. He was active in several literary societies, member of the glee club, class president, member of the Phi Gamma Delta fraternity, a nearly unbeatable checker player, and star of both the baseball and football teams.

He broke into pro ball in 1899 with the Taunton (Massachusetts) club of the New England League, getting into 17 games, posting a 5–2 record, and earning $90 a month—or supposedly, for he saw little of it as the team gradually went broke.

In 1900, the nineteen-year-old Mathewson, still determined to make a go of it in professional baseball (if he hadn't made it, he had already decided on a fallback career in forestry, an occupation "best suited to my particular tastes"), was with the Norfolk (Virginia) club in the Virginia League. Here he took his first toehold on the legend to be. In little over half a season he mounted a 20–2 record, which is about as fancy as it gets. A 20–2 won-lost record never goes unnoticed, whether it be deep in the Amazon Jungle, high among Himalayan slopes, or in Norfolk, Virginia. By the end of July Mathewson was in New York, getting a look-see from the Giants. If they kept him, the Giants would pay Norfolk $1,500.

"Mathewson talks like a Harvard graduate, looks like an actor, acts like a businessman, and impresses you like an all-around gentleman."

The storybook hero did not start in storybook style, however. He got into six games with the Giants and showed an 0–3 record. Rather than pay the $1,500, the Giants returned him to Norfolk. The man who was to become the greatest pitcher of his time, maybe of all time, was drifting. Or so he thought. Without informing him, Norfolk sold his contract to the Cincinnati Reds. Still unaware of the transaction, Mathewson agreed to an offer he received from Connie Mack, manager of the Philadelphia club of the newly formed American League.

A few weeks later Mathewson received "a red-hot communication" from Andrew Freedman, owner of the Giants, summoning him to New York. There Christy was informed that Norfolk had sold him to Cincinnati and Cincinnati to New York; he also received a stern lecture laced with threats. He was told that he was the

Posing at the Polo Grounds in 1912

property of the Giants, that the freshly hatched American League wouldn't last three months, and that any player who joined the upstarts would be blacklisted. If he persisted in honoring his agreement with Mack, Mathewson was warned, Freedman would bring suit against the young pitcher.

Thoroughly intimidated and chagrined, Christy wrote to Mack explaining the situation. Connie decided not to pursue it (thus losing the opportunity of hav-

ing a pitching staff of Rube Waddell, Eddie Plank, Chief Bender, and Christy Mathewson, a four-man rotation capable of 100 victories among them in any given year).

So Mathewson was now a New York Giant and soon was working for the manager with whom his name was to be forever linked, John J. McGraw.

There is no more improbable relationship in all of baseball than the one that developed between the tall, gentlemanly, almost aristocratic Mathewson and the short, often crude and blasphemous McGraw, who thought nothing of verbally crucifying a player for mental mistakes on the ball field. Given the backgrounds and temperaments of the two men, even a rudimentary friendship would have seemed unlikely. Nevertheless, a bond grew between them (and their wives; the two couples even shared an apartment one summer in New York) that lasted until Mathewson's untimely death in 1925. The childless McGraw looked upon Mathewson as a son, while nothing that McGraw ever did—not the profanity, sarcasm, and invective he hurled at offending players—could diminish the big pitcher's loyalty, respect, and admiration.

McGraw got along with his 30-game winner because Mathewson, despite his genteel demeanor, was as gritty and hard-bitten a competitor as his skipper. Both were grimly intent on winning, and though they may have used different vehicles, both were fixed on the same destination. In particular, Mathewson respected McGraw's mastery of what both regarded as a highly sophisticated game.

In 1901, his first full season, Mathewson had a 20–17 record for a team that won just 52 games and finished seventh.

"In all," he later wrote, "I made quite a reputation as a young pitcher of promise." He was at that time receiving a salary of $1,500 a year "and had been well content." His teammates, however, began badgering him into asking for more money, pointing out to him that more and more people were turning out to see him pitch and that he "ought to shake Freedman down for a good increase."

When Mathewson broached the subject of more money to the owner, Freedman bought him two new suits, "which I needed and which was a substantial item from my point of view." The following year, Mathewson "shook down" Freedman for a $3,500 salary.

Pitching for an even worse Giant team in 1902, Mathewson had a 14–17 record. This was the year McGraw took over as

Warming up at the Polo Grounds

manager in midseason, beginning his 31-year tenure as Giants skipper.

A year later Mathewson attained stardom with a 30–13 record. It marked the beginning of 12 straight years of over 20 victories, including eight of 25 or better and four of 30 or better. He averaged 26 wins per season over that 12-year span.

In 1904 Mathewson was 33–12, a year later 31–9, giving him three consecutive 30-game seasons (a record he shares with Grover Cleveland Alexander). That 1905 season was one of Christy's greatest; his pitching was, as one writer put it, "impossibly good." He led in victories, winning percentage (.795), earned run average (1.27), strikeouts (206), and shutouts (9). And then that fall, against the Philadelphia Athletics, he raised an ensign of sterling performance that established an all-time standard for World Series play. In the space of six days—between October 9 and 14—he started and completed

Mathewson *(right)* with John McGraw

three shutouts, allowing but 14 hits and one base on balls in 27 innings. "It was," Mathewson said, "the achievement which stands out in my memory above all others."

He was now a national hero, and not just for his work on the mound but for the personal distinction he projected and how he was perceived by the public. He was praised and lionized in newspapers and magazines; songs were written about him; he was even saluted from the pulpits as a glorious prototype. Not only was he dazzling them in the ball yards of America with his wizardry, but he was at the same time bringing "respectability" to the national game, to a profession often characterized as an outlet for ruffians and drunkards. (If his mother had hoped he would be a preacher, then at least he had become, to a segment of the public anyway, something of a missionary in the jungles of professional baseball.) Christy's image grew to such proportions of purity that his wife was finally constrained to mildly protest that her husband was not "a goody-goody." (Indeed, Christy was known to smoke cigars, occasionally rattle some dice with his teammates, and at fully ripened moments paint the air blue with certain well-chosen epithets.)

The image never blurred or faltered, not for a moment. Mathewson's natural aloofness, like Joe DiMaggio's years later, only added to his grandeur and his mystique. He was known to pull down window shades on trains to block out the view of the crowds who had gathered on station platforms to catch a glimpse of him. He could walk through throngs of admirers "like he was striding alone on an empty beach," according to Chief Meyers, his catcher. He was a hard man to get to know, another teammate said; but once you got past the chill, "he was truly a good and loyal friend."

But it all meant nothing without those victories, those methodical year-in, year-out performances. There were no-hitters, against St. Louis in 1901 and Chicago in 1905, and in 1913, from June 19 to July 18, he worked 68 consecutive innings without giving up a base on balls. That season he pitched 306 innings and walked just 21, and the following year it was 312 innings and 23 walks.

In 1908 Mathewson reached a crescendo, with 37 wins against 11 losses. Fighting for a pennant, ultimately lost by one game to the Cubs (it was the year of the "Merkle boner," which cost the Giants a September victory over the Cubs), McGraw worked his twenty-eight-year-old ace 390 innings, in which Matty posted a 1.43 ERA, fanned 259, and delivered 12 shutouts. It was his fourth season of 30 or more wins, a record for the twentieth century, one of those records that seems permanently secure from assault.

A year later he was 25–6, with his lowest ERA ever, 1.14, third-lowest in National League history (to Three Finger Brown's 1.04 in 1906 and Bob Gibson's 1.12 in 1968). It went on for another five years, with 27 wins in 1910, 26 in 1911, 23 in 1912, 25 in 1913, and 24 in 1914.

In 1914, Mathewson wrote of himself, "At one time I had very fair speed . . . but I was never what would be technically known as a speed pitcher. Doubtless my curve was really my best ball. At least it was always my favorite. The slow ball which I have used so often and termed the 'fade away' was always a part of my natural mechanical gifts . . . I have never used the spitball." (The latter was a legal pitch in Mathewson's time.)

The origins of the "fade away," one of the pitches that not only made him nearly invincible but that helped to create the Mathewson mystique, are somewhat uncertain, though it is known that he was throwing it when he was with Taunton in 1899. Not uncommon today, the pitch was positively exotic back then. It was delivered with a reverse twist of the wrist and in essence was a screwball, breaking in on a right-handed batter and away from a left-handed. Very few pitchers threw it in those days, none of them with Mathewson's mastery. Added to his fast ball and curve, it gave him perhaps the most potent pitching arsenal in baseball history—and he threw all three with delicately controlled precision.

In 1915, the now thirty-five-year-old icon dropped to an 8–14 record. His career as an active player was now clearly drawing to a close. The following July, after appearing in just 13 games and struggling to a 3–4 record, Mathewson was traded to Cincinnati, where he had been offered the manager's job.

Mathewson pitched once for the Reds, winning, then retired as an active player. He left behind a lifetime 373–188 won-lost record, a victory total later tied by Grover Cleveland Alexander (that tie for the all-time leadership for victories in the National League remains one of baseball's most intriguing statistics). Matty's lifetime ERA of 2.13 is second lowest in league history, to Brown's 2.06, while his 83 shutouts are third in major-league history, to Walter Johnson's 110 and Alexander's 90.

Mathewson managed the Reds until late August 1918, when he left to join the military. He went in as a captain in the Army Chemical Warfare Division. In this capacity, he inhaled some poison gas (either in a training session or while inspecting the trenches in France soon after the armistice), severely damaging his lungs.

After spending some time in the hospital, he seemed to have recovered. He returned to the Giants in 1919 as a coach for McGraw, but his health soon began to deteriorate; tuberculosis was diagnosed. He moved with his family to Saranac Lake in New York's Adirondack Mountains, location of a world-famous sanitorium. By the spring of 1925 his condition began to worsen. He coughed and gasped away the summer, and on October 7, 1925, he died, two months after his forty-fifth birthday.

The tributes that poured in after his death were lavish in praise of the man and the pitcher. Among them was the following: "He had proved you could play professional baseball and remain a gentleman."

"Eddie Plank was a hard man to know."

EDDIE PLANK

If you were touring the Gettysburg battlefield in autumn or winter back in the first quarter of the century, your tour guide might have been a lean, soft-spoken, quite reserved man whose face seldom changed expression. He would tell you about Cemetery Ridge and Little Round Top, show you where Pickett's doomed Confederates lined up for their charge, where Lincoln stood while making his memorable two-minute address. He could have told you about the generals, about Meade and Lee and Stuart and Longstreet, and, if he wanted to, about some other American notables, like Connie Mack, Ty Cobb, and Christy Mathewson, for this poker-faced fellow who used his words in such careful measurement was Eddie Plank, the gifted southpaw of the Philadelphia Athletics.

It should have been no surprise to anyone that Eddie chose to return to Gettysburg after each season, for he was a man of precise and unvarying habits, and the historic little farm town was where he had been born (on August 31, 1875),

raised on the family farm, gone to college (Gettysburg College), and where he died at the age of fifty on February 24, 1926. In between, he pitched in the American League for 16 years (plus one year in the Federal League) and won 305 games, most of them for Connie Mack and the Philadelphia Athletics, whom he joined straight out of college in 1901.

A tireless and methodical worker, Plank, who was described as throwing "with a sweeping crossfire motion," was a 20-game winner eight times, with peaks of 26 in 1904 and 1912. His 64 lifetime shutouts place him fifth on the all-time list, excusably behind those standard-brand record holders Walter Johnson, Grover Cleveland Alexander, Christy Mathewson, and Cy Young.

There was never a steadier or more dependable pitcher, nor a more self-effacing one. He had none of the flamboyance of his fireballing left-handed teammate Rube Waddell; Eddie, in fact, seems to have been most frugal at presenting himself. Sixteen years on the big-league scene and barely a word or an anecdote left behind, only those sterling numbers in the record books to attest to his uncompromising fidelity to his craft. It is as if his every footprint filled in the moment he marked it, and that when he died his very shadow swam after him to the grave.

But when Eddie was on the mound, he was much noticed and deeply admired. Bob Shawkey, a right-handed pitcher who came to the big leagues with the Athletics in 1913 and later starred with the Yankees in the 1920s, called Plank "one of the greatest left-handers that ever pitched. He had a good curve ball and fast ball, and he knew where he was throwing that ball." But Eddie "was a hard man to know," Shawkey said. "I wouldn't say he was unfriendly, but he wasn't particularly friendly either. He was a loner, always keeping to himself. On road trips the guys would sit around the hotel lobby or go out to hoist a couple, but you never saw Eddie. Mr. Mack, who always treated everybody just right, seemed to understand him. He called him 'Edward.' He'd tell him, 'Edward, you're pitching today,' and that would be that. No instructions, no words of wisdom. Just send him out there. When it came to the craft, I think Mr. Mack realized that Eddie didn't need any help."

Smoky Joe Wood, the Red Sox ace right-hander, recalled Plank on the mound this way: "Plank was very studious out there. He used to pitch to spots, more so than most fellows of the day, I would say. They do that more today, but Eddie Plank was doing it back then, in the first decade of the century, and doing it very well."

Eddie's teammate, the astute second baseman Eddie Collins, saw Plank as something of the farm-boy psycholo-gist on the mound. "He fidgeted around a lot on the mound," Collins said. "I think it was a deliberate part of his technique, keeping the batters off balance. Then he'd fire a pitch right into his target. His control was superb."

Collins gives this more detailed description of the Plank technique:

Plank's favorite situation was two men on and a slugger up. The better

Eddie Plank

"Plank was very studious out there."

the hitter the better Eddie liked it. For, if a man had a reputation to uphold, the fans would urge him on, and he would be aching to hit. Plank would fuss and fuddle with the ball, with his shoes, and then try to talk with the umpire. . . . Then he'd dish up something the batter couldn't reach with two bats, would follow that with an equally wild pitch— inside. Probably the next would be a twister the batter could reach, but could not straighten out. A couple of fouls, and he would wink knowingly at me. Then he would attempt to pick off the base runners, which he frequently did. Then, suddenly, Plank would turn his attention to the fretting batter again, who would, in all probability pop up in disgust.

Plank came to professional baseball comparatively late. He enrolled in Gettysburg College at the age of twenty-one and soon was pitching for the school team. He became a renowned college pitcher, mowing down the opposition with ease—except when working against Bucknell, where his opponent was that school's ace, Christy Mathewson. Matty generally bested him, a pattern that continued later in the 1905 World Series when Mathewson beat him 3–0 in the opener and again in the 1913 Series when Christy again beat him 3–0 in 10 innings in game two. Eddie finally beat his old nemesis 3–1 in the fifth and final game.

On graduation from college, Plank joined the Athletics. The year was 1901, Year One in the history of the American League. The twenty-five-year-old rookie was impressive, and Connie kept him. Eddie gave Mack a solid 17–11 season and took off from there, helping the Athletics to six pennants, in 1902 (when there

was no World Series), 1905, 1910, 1911, 1913, and 1914. Eddie's World Series record was 2–5, despite an earned run average of 1.15 for 55 innings of work (he was shut out four times, twice by scores of 1–0).

When asked to compare Plank and Rube Waddell, Athletics right-hander Jack Coombs replied, "Now, get me right. Waddell may have had a sharper-breaking curve and more speed, but when it comes down to a question of brain combined with ability and real worth to a team, there never was a pitcher the superior of Ed Plank."

The quiet man had his handful of quirks. One was that within a pitcher's system there lay a finite allotment of pitches and that when the supply was depleted the pitcher was finished. There is no doubt a grounding of logic in this, but Eddie believed it fervently enough to permit himself the merest minimum of warmup pitches before a start, in the belief that even these were part of the "supply." He believed, too, that having his picture taken on the day of a start presaged bad luck.

Eddie was also known to talk aloud to himself on the mound, particularly from the seventh inning on, when he began counting out the batters. "Nine to get," he'd say, loud enough to be heard by his infielders. "Eight to get." And so on. This was apparently no affectation. "I'm not even sure he was aware we could hear him," Collins said. "He concentrated out there like a hypnotist."

In 1914, the Federal League opened up shop in competition with the established major leagues. In 1915, Plank, wanting to take advantage of the higher salaries the upstarts were offering, obtained his release from the Athletics and joined the

Three of Connie Mack's stalwarts. *Left to right:* first baseman Harry Davis, pitcher Jack Coombs, and Eddie Plank.

new league's St. Louis club. At the age of forty, Eddie was 21–11 in the Federal League. When the new confection dissolved after the 1915 season, he returned to the American League, with the St. Louis Browns. In his final two seasons, 1916 and 1917, he was 16–15 and 5–6. After the 1917 season he was sold to the Yankees, but at the age of forty-two he felt he had had enough baseball and retired to his Pennsylvania farm.

He kept his hand in by pitching semi-pro ball for several years, well enough for the Yankees to try and coax him back. But Eddie was permanently settled now.

On February 20, 1926, Plank suffered a paralytic stroke and died in Gettysburg four days later.

Years later, when discussing the great triumvirate of left-handers he had managed—Waddell, Plank, and later, Lefty Grove—Connie Mack would maintain that Rube was the best of them. "Although," the old man added, "when there was a game I absolutely had to win, Edward was the man I would send out there."

With "Edward's" lifetime record of 305–181, Connie's choice was usually the correct one.

Mordecai Peter Centennial Three Finger Brown

"THREE FINGER" BROWN

If there was no question that Christy Mathewson was the National League's best pitcher during the century's opening decade, then neither was there any question about who was second-best. His name was Mordecai Peter Centennial Brown (the Centennial was for being born in the centennial year of 1876), but he was more commonly known as "Three Finger." (They also called him "Miner" because as a teenager he had worked in the mines of his hometown, Nyesville, Indiana, where he was born on October 19, 1876.)

Brown was seven years old when he suffered the accident that mangled his right hand, altered his personal destiny, and helped establish a dynasty for the Chicago Cubs. The boy was visiting an uncle's farm when he somehow got his hand caught in a corn shredder, and by the time he snatched it back he had lost most of his index finger and suffered serious injuries to his pinky and thumb. Little Mordecai may have sobbed and howled with pain, and his parents may

have been heartsick, but this was clearly a case of fate deciding that it wanted, after all, this boy to be a big-league pitcher.

Brown never possessed blazing speed on the mound, but what the odd configuration of his right hand gave him was a curve ball with an exceedingly sharp downward break. Mathewson described Brown's curve as "big" and said that Three Finger had "absolute control" of it. Mathewson also called Brown "a wonderful fielder and sure death on bunts." While this ability may not loom as large in today's game, back then, in the dead-ball era, the bunt was a common offensive tactic and the pitcher an important defensive player. Brown, according to Mathewson, was one of the best.

While Mathewson was unquestionably the league's premier pitcher, in head-to-head matchups with Brown, Three Finger came out on top, 13–11.

In 1898 Brown was playing semipro ball on the open fields of Indiana. He was a third baseman then. One day the club's

27

pitcher injured his arm and Mordecai was pressed into service. His good fast ball and swooping hooks sealed his destiny: He was thereafter a pitcher.

In 1901 Brown signed to pitch for Terre Haute (Indiana) in the Three-I League. A 23–8 record earned him a promotion to Omaha of the Western League, where he was 27–15. That win total perked the interest of the St. Louis Cardinals, who purchased him and brought him to the big leagues in 1903.

Brown posted a 9–13 rookie year for a last-place club that won only 43 games. Despite a 2.60 earned run average, lowest on the team and one of the best in the league, the Cardinals traded him to the Cubs after the season. It was said the Cardinals felt that Brown's battered right hand was a handicap that would prevent him from becoming a star pitcher. The Cardinals were exactly wrong.

Brown was 15–10 with the Cubs in 1904, with an ERA of 1.84, third-lowest in the league. The following year he made it to the brink of stardom with an 18–12 record and 2.17 ERA, fifth-best in the league.

In 1906 Brown and the Cubs began an impressive run of success. It was a record-making year all around, the Cubs setting a major-league record with 116 wins and Brown a National League standard with a 1.04 ERA. His record was 26–6, and he led the league with 10 shutouts, headlining a staff that logged a collective 1.76 ERA.

This was the team of Tinker, Evers, and Chance, the crack infield (along with third baseman Harry Steinfeldt) that picked up the ground balls that Brown threw. In the World Series, in which the Cubs were upset by their crosstown rivals, the White Sox, Brown was 1–2, pitching a two-hit shutout in game four.

Three Finger Brown

Chicago won the pennant again in 1907, with Brown shaping a 20–6 record, 1.39 ERA, and six shutouts, and then adding another shutout over Ty Cobb's Tigers in the Cubs' World Series victory.

In 1908 the methodical Brown reached his personal victory high, with a 29–9 season, a 1.47 ERA (second to Mathewson's 1.43), and nine shutouts. He was 2–0 (including a shutout) in the World Series as the Cubs again defeated the Tigers for the championship.

But before the Cubs could get into that World Series they had to play one of the most emotionally charged baseball games of all time.

The Cubs and Giants had put on a bruising battle for the pennant, and in the heat of the homestretch fury came "Merkle's boner." This took place in the Polo Grounds on September 22, and it deprived the Giants of a victory over the Cubs, a victory they appeared to have sealed up. The incident occurred when base runner Fred Merkle failed to touch second base after what should have been a game-winning hit, thereby nullifying the run. Thinking their team had won, the partisan New York crowd swarmed onto the field after the hit; it was impossible to clear the field to resume play, and the game was declared a tie.

When the Giants and Cubs finished the season with identical 98–55 records, the game was ordered replayed at the Polo Grounds on October 8. The National League pennant would go to the winner.

The Polo Grounds had been sold out early, and fans were sitting on the elevated tracks overlooking the field, preventing the trains from running. When the fire department drove them off the tracks with high-pressure hoses, the incensed fans set fire to the outfield fences,

Fred Merkle, the man who didn't touch second base

hoping to break through, but were driven off by mounted police. The Cubs, recipients of numerous death threats since their arrival in the city, sat in a dugout ringed with policemen. In this heady atmosphere a pennant race was to be decided.

Because Brown had worked in 11 of the Cubs' previous 14 games, starting and relieving, skipper Frank Chance gave the crucial start to lefty Jack Pfiester. The Giant starter was, inevitably, Mathewson, whom Brown describes appearing on the field from out of the center-field clubhouse: "I can still see Christy Mathewson making his lordly entrance. He'd always wait until about ten minutes before game time, then he'd come from the clubhouse across the field in a long linen duster like auto drivers wore in

The Chicago Cubs in pregame workout at West Side Park in 1908

those days, and at every step the crowd would yell louder and louder. This day they split the air."

When Pfiester allowed a run in the bottom of the first and had two men on, Chance, knowing that to give Matty more than a few runs could be fatal, called in Brown.

Three Finger had to come in from the bullpen in right-center field. He needed a police escort to get through the SRO crowd lining the outfield. He recalled being cursed and threatened, and responding, "Get the hell out of the way."

Pitching in "as near a lunatic asylum as I ever saw," Brown absorbed the pressure like a sponge and held the Giants to four hits and one run for the rest of the game. His teammates roughed up Mathewson for four runs in the top of the third, and that was it, a 4–2 win and a Chicago pennant.

The Cubs had to leave New York under police escort.

In 1909 Brown was 27–9, with a 1.31 ERA and eight shutouts. He now had a four-year record of 102 wins against just 30 losses. In 1910 he was 25–14, with a 1.86 ERA and seven shutouts, helping the Cubs to their fourth pennant in five years. He was 1–2 in the World Series, which the Cubs lost to the Philadelphia Athletics.

Brown's sixth consecutive, and final, 20-game season came in 1911, when he was 21–11.

A knee injury held him to a 5–6 record

in 1912. In 1913 he was traded to Cincinnati, where he rang up an 11–12 record. In 1914 and 1915 he played in the newly formed Federal League, which folded after two years.

In 1916, Three Finger, now thirty-nine years old, returned to the scene of past glories, signing once more with the Cubs. But those glories were now securely past. He got into just 12 games and had a 2–3 record. In his final big-league start, on Labor Day, he was matched with Mathewson, now managing Cincinnati, who was also making his farewell appearance. The two former top aces staggered and stumbled their way through a 10–8 game, which Mathewson won, and simultaneously ended their careers.

Mordecai Peter Centennial (Three Finger) Brown left the major leagues with a 208–111 record, 2.06 lifetime ERA (the lowest of any National League pitcher), and those six exquisitely pitched seasons between 1906 and 1911. His 1.04 ERA in 1906 remains the lowest single-season figure in National League history.

Brown died in Terre Haute, Indiana, on February 14, 1948.

Brown in 1908. Note the stub of forefinger.

Ed Walsh

ED WALSH

One of Ed Walsh's contemporaries remembered the great Chicago White Sox right-hander this way: "Big, strong, good-looking guy. He'd work as often as you asked him to. Never complained, never seemed to get tired. Sometimes they'd come in for a four-game series and you'd see him in every game, starting and relieving, relieving and starting. Of course you can't do that for very long."

Ed Walsh did not do it for very long (comparatively speaking); but considering the workload handed him and his ready acceptance of it, he did do it for an impressively long time. His strength, stamina, and resilience must have been remarkable; statistically, it was more remarkable than any other twentieth-century pitcher, for none has ever topped Walsh's 465 innings pitched in 1908.

The man who was to become known as "the Spit Ball King" (a legal pitch back then) was born on May 14, 1881, in Plains, Pennsylvania, a small town in the heart of eastern Pennsylvania's anthracite country (a few miles south of Factoryville, where Christy Mathewson was born the previous August).

One of 10 boys in a family of 13, Ed took what might be described as the foredoomed opportunity of all the young men of Plains—work in the mines. He probably would have spent his working life in these grimy manmade corridors if not for his "recreation"—playing baseball.

Even when he was a youngster, people remarked about his "marvelous build," his "iron constitution," his arm "like chilled steel." Pitching semipro ball on Sundays, Walsh had a fast ball that hummed loud enough to be heard all the way to Meriden, Connecticut, which offered him a contract to join its club in the Connecticut League. Seeing the opportunity to leave the underground forever, Walsh accepted the $125-per-month offer and in July 1902 entered professional baseball.

He was 15–5 for his half season's work with Meriden. He was 11–10 midway through the next season when he was sold to Newark, then in the Eastern League. He finished up there with a 9–5 record, pitching with a relentless determination, for, as he said, "The shadow of the mines was on me. It was either make good or back to the mines."

The "miner pitcher" (as he was known) was recommended to the Boston Red Sox, but they turned him down because they already had an abundance of quality pitching (a state of affairs that will no doubt fall wistfully on the sensibilities of latter-day Red Sox fans). So "Big Ed" (at 6'1" he was big for his time) was sold to the Chicago White Sox.

Walsh started off modestly with the White Sox, with records of 6–3 and 8–3 in 1904 and 1905. But during these years he had begun experimenting on the side-

Ed Walsh. "Big, strong, good-looking guy."

lines with the spitball. "From the very first," he said, "the spitball appealed to me as a wonderfully effective" pitch.

Walsh was not the inventor of this damp delivery, but he soon became its most brilliant exponent. According to one writer of the day, "Walsh took the spitball when it was at best a poor experiment, a shadow of its present self, and with his strength and skill and patient application he made of it a wonder, the marvel of the baseball world," the "terror of every batting star."

To Walsh, the pitch, which was sometimes described as "a black art" and a delivery of "strange fantasies," was simple and straightforward. There were just two components to its mastery: speed and practice. "It is pitched," he said, "with the first two fingers wet. The friction of these two fingers gives it a peculiar spiral motion, and this motion, coupled with the great speed with which it is thrown, causes it to break sharply before it crosses the plate."

Walsh, who had caught some attention in 1905 by pitching two complete-game wins over Boston on September 26, began riding his spitter to success in 1906. He was 17–13 that year, leading the league with 10 shutouts. His pitching helped the White Sox to win the pennant, and in the World Series he defeated the Chicago Cubs twice as the Sox upset their highly favored opponents in the only all-Chicago World Series ever played.

A year later Walsh was 24–18, with a league-leading 1.60 earned run average. It was in this season that the twenty-six-year-old right-hander began demonstrating the further reaches of his endurance. He started 46 times, completed 37 games, appeared 56 times overall, and worked 419 innings, leading in each category.

The man who pitched 465 innings in 1908

Walsh *(left)* and Addie Joss

The following season he turned in a summer of monumental work.

In 1908 Walsh started 49 games, completed 42, appeared in a total of 66 games, won 40, lost 15, pitched his prodigious 465 innings, fanned 269, had 12 shutouts, and had an ERA of 1.42. Despite this Herculean work, the White Sox did not win the pennant, finishing third 1½ games behind Detroit.

Making Walsh's 1908 season even more amazing is the fact that he was toiling for one of the most feeble offensive clubs ever. The White Sox batted .224 that year, hitting just three home runs all season (one of which was struck by Big Ed himself). It is, of course, true that this was the dead-ball era and the league as a whole batted .239 and hit only 116 home runs, but the White Sox attack was more moribund than most, and for a man to win 40 games—improbable under any circumstances—with a club that batted .224 is astonishing.

It is also true that Walsh worked in an era when pitchers delivered more innings and more complete games. Nevertheless, the winning total next high to Walsh's 40 was 24, the next high in innings to his 465 was 325, and the next high to his 42 complete games was 30. Walsh's year bordered on the superhuman, regardless of his era.

Coming down the stretch that year, Walsh again pitched and won a doubleheader, against Boston on September 29. In fact, over the last eight days of a torrid three-way pennant race with Detroit and Cleveland, Big Ed worked in six games, including his doubleheader wins.

Perhaps his most celebrated game, and one of the greatest pitching confrontations ever, took place against Cleveland's Addie Joss on October 2. With the American League pennant swirling tantalizingly near, Walsh and Joss pitched to sublime heights. For Joss it was a perfect game, suffocating Walsh's three-hit, 15-strikeout effort with a 1–0 victory.

Big Ed had reached his peak in 1908. He leveled off to 15–11 in 1909 and 18–20 a year later. The latter year saw him in a most curious juxtaposition of league leads: in both losses (20) and ERA (1.27). How can a man log so low an earned run average and still lose 20 games? Well, Ed was surrounded by culprits—the 1910 White Sox batted a pallid .212, still the lowest team batting average in the twentieth century.

Walsh came back with a 27–18 record in 1911 (including a no-hitter against Boston on August 27) and 27–17 in 1912, pitching 393 innings in the latter year.

After that, the erosion caused by almost a decade of tireless pitching gradually brought his career to a close. He was 8–3 in 1913, then petered out over the next three seasons. His final won-lost record was 195–126, with the lowest lifetime earned run average in history—1.82 for nearly 3,000 innings. His 40 wins in 1908 stand second in this century only to Jack Chesbro's 41 in 1904.

A 1913 article painted this homey portrait of Walsh: "As I have known him Ed Walsh, the man, kindly, courteous, considerate, loyal to his friends, and to himself, simple, unaffected, patient in adversity, unspoiled by prosperity, is in all respects equal to Ed Walsh, the ballplayer, and one of the greatest pitchers the game has ever known."

Walsh died in Pompano Beach, Florida, on May 26, 1959, just after his seventy-eighth birthday.

Walter Johnson: "You knew what was coming. But so what?"

WALTER JOHNSON

His fast balls were described with the kind of awe accorded comet sightings, and the analogy does not seem unreasonable, for of all major-league pitchers, Walter Johnson has left behind the most majestic cosmic imprint. Never mind that he was modest and gentle and soft-spoken, that he was kind of heart and noble of character. It's fine, but ultimately none of it matters. When you are talking about Walter Johnson you are talking about a fast ball, one so fast that for nearly two decades it was almost as if nobody else threw one, so fast that today tales of its velocity can strain one's credulity.

Walter's contemporaries claimed he could fire that little bullet of his with such snappy swiftness that there were times when it seemed to disappear into thin air, as if buzzing off into some dimension all its own, and sometimes so fast that you could "*hear* it shoot by." Hear it? Well, that wasn't impossible, because in those less extravagant days baseballs were often left in play even with slightly torn covers, and maybe it was one of these that those fervent witnesses heard hissing through the strike zone. (If that is indeed the answer, then it was still only the torn covers thrown by Walter that made little whispers of sound in passage.)

Those old-timers, their minds luminous with the memories of Mathewson's patrician artistry, fairly vibrated with recollections of Walter's speed. In his day, Johnson assumed a sort of mythic, larger-than-life status, a grandeur achieved only by Ruth; they were baseball's preeminent symbols of its most enthralling elements: speed and power.

This prime example of mythology, American style, was born right in the heart of the continent, in Humboldt, Kansas, on November 6, 1887. He spent the first 14 years of his life there, working on his father's farm, developing his sturdy physique, growing tall, broad of shoulder, and, most crucially, long of arm. Those arms would grow to unusual length, and it was of course that right one that he would swing behind him and then

New man in town. Walter Johnson arrives in Washington in 1907.

In 1907, Walter, not yet twenty years old, was working in Weiser, Idaho, in the western part of the state, digging postholes for the Weiser Telephone Company. He was also pitching for the company's baseball team, to whose opponents he must have seemed like something from another planet. Imagine the amateurs of western Idaho trying to get around on those low-slung bullets. (Walter would be in the major leagues before the leaves turned that year, and after one look Ty Cobb would say, "That busher throws the fastest pitch I've ever seen.")

Walter's fast ball was duly appreciated by the rugged folk of Weiser, and he soon

Cliff Blankenship, the Washington Senators catcher who corralled Walter.

hurl forward to "buggy whip" the ball on its brief, searing journey. That was the word most commonly used to describe the Johnson delivery: "buggy whip." It was a sidearm delivery; on some old film footage it looks almost underhand. Another feature of those intriguing old films is seeing that Walter had no follow-through. His right foot never moves; it remains behind him all the time, instead of being used to help thrust him forward. In other words, if those films are representative, Walter pitched entirely with his arm.

The lure of western riches brought the Johnson family to California in 1901. They didn't strike gold, but they did earn a decent living supplying mules to oil-field workers.

became quite a local hero, to the extent, he recalled, that "people began calling me 'pardner' instead of 'sonny.' "

The Walter Johnson legend properly begins with the anonymous traveling salesman who saw him pitch and wrote to the Washington Senators describing this wondrous experience in a most extravagant way. One of the letters read, in part: "He throws the ball so fast it's like a little white bullet going down to the catcher." In another, he said: "He knows where his pitch is going. Otherwise, there would be dead bodies scattered all over Idaho." The Senators, located in a city where hyperbole was not unknown, were pardonably skeptical.

Washington catcher Cliff Blankenship was injured at this time and not playing, so the club sent him out west to scout outfielder Clyde Milan, then with the Wichita club. While he was out there, Cliff was told, he might as well have a look at the fellow in Idaho.

Blankenship acquired Milan (who became a fine outfielder for the club over the next 15 years) and went on to Weiser. For some reason, he didn't get a chance to see Walter pitch, but tales of the young man's abilities were so stirring that Blankenship decided to make an offer: a $100 bill and $350 a month for the rest of the season (this was sometime in late July).

When the people of Weiser heard about this, they made a counteroffer: If he would stay they would buy him a cigar stand and set him up in business. Quite a tribute to the young man; more specifically, to his fast ball. A grateful Walter turned them down. "I was young," he said, "and wanted to see things."

So Walter Perry Johnson boarded a train and headed East, for the nation's

"The Big Train"

capital, where he would soon establish himself as one of the premier attractions of that city of great men and noble monuments. He was in his way more representative of his country than anyone else in that city of elected representatives, a genuine embodiment of the bruited American ethos, for Walter was filled with strength and might and generosity. His gaze was direct, his features frank and open. There was neither guile nor malice in Walter, not in the way he lived or in the way he pitched. Certainly not in the way he pitched.

"He only had the one pitch," Cleveland shortstop Roger Peckinpaugh said. "You knew what was coming. But so what?"

The only unfortunate aspect of Walter's trip East was that it was to Washington (unfortunate in particular to those romantics who daydream about records), for poor Walter was hitching himself to the slowest wagon in the league. The American League's strong teams were then Boston, Detroit, and Philadelphia. Washington was a perennial tail-ender, usually found among the cobwebs of the standings, a team of anemic batting averages and parsimonious scoring. But Walter never complained; it was not in his nature, and this stoicism only helped foster his nobility and build his legend.

In any event, one might fairly ask, how much better could his record have been? After all, we're talking about somebody who won 25 games or better for seven straight years and 20 or better for 10 straight years. In 1912–13 he won 68 and lost just 19. His 1913 season, when he was 36–7, with a 1.09 earned run average, 11 shutouts, 243 strikeouts, and 38 walks in 346 innings, may have been the greatest single season any pitcher has ever had.

In his first partial season, Walter had a taste of what was coming. He pitched extraordinarily well, with a 1.87 ERA for 110 innings, and found himself 5–9 when it was over. He got another heavy dose of humility two years later, when his last-place teammates batted .223 and albatrossed him with a 13–25 record.

The year before, in 1908, Walter had given a dazzling display of zip and stamina when he shut out the Yankees on September 4, 5, and 7. Even in an age when pitchers went to the hill with greater frequency than they do today, this is pretty heady stuff.

We'll never know just how fast Walter burned them in, though the record books

Walter Johnson

give us a generous idea. For instance, the big boy led in strikeouts 12 times, including eight years in a row (1912–1919). This is the mark of super speed.

They called him "the Big Train" and "Barney." Both nicknames were for speed—Barney Oldfield was then America's ace race-car driver. In baseball, Walter was the epitome of speed, and probably always will be, as Ruth will forever be the symbol of the home run, Maris and Aaron notwithstanding.

In 1913, Walter found a surefire way of winning, and never mind the weak sisters around him. In that year, statistically his greatest, he established a major-league record (since broken by Don Drysdale) of 55⅔ consecutive scoreless innings, the equivalent of better than six straight shutouts. No one, in fact, has pitched more shutouts than Johnson—110, with 38 of them won by 1–0 scores (he lost 26 by the same score).

In 1912, he won 16 straight games, still the American League record (tied three times, by Joe Wood that same year, Lefty Grove in 1931, and Schoolboy Rowe in 1934). On July 1, 1920, he pitched his only no-hitter, against the Red Sox.

Patiently, tirelessly, Walter kept slinging his fast balls. World War I came and went, then the lively ball arrived, and Walter kept firing, a living legend now, widely beloved and respected. All who watched him, who played with or against him, knew that they were privileged.

After 17 years, Walter had done it all, led over and over again in all the categories vital to a pitcher. One thing, however, had eluded him—a World Series. But in 1924 it finally happened, Washington winning its first pennant by two games over the Yankees. Walter at last had the hitters with him, as Goose Goslin, Sam

Johnson in 1925

Rice, Joe Judge, and second baseman–manager Bucky Harris sparked the lineup. And on the mound it was, as ever, Walter Johnson. At the age of thirty-six, after four years of not winning 20, Walter was the best pitcher in the American League, leading in wins (23–7), ERA (2.72), strikeouts (158), and shutouts (6).

So the pageant of the World Series, always brightly colored with expectations to begin with, was enhanced even more by the presence of a tremendously sentimental figure. And with the opposition being the New York Giants of John J. McGraw—baseball's reigning lords, with four straight pennants—the drama had additional spice.

But to the dismay of the sentimental-

Manager of the Washington Senators

ists, Johnson started the opening game and lost 4–3 in 12 innings. He started the fifth game and lost again, 6–2, given a good rattling by McGraw's heavy gunners.

But there was to be a seventh game. In careers as long and as heroic as Johnson's, there almost inevitably comes that one purely theatrical moment, that compelling blend of romance and drama that is first obligatory and then revelatory.

The Series had bounced back and forth, and now here was game seven, in Washington. Johnson, having gone the route two days before, did not start, but he was ready if called upon. The call came in the top of the ninth with the score tied 3–3. Walter, modest to the end, said, "I'll always believe that Harris gambled on me because of sentiment." Possible, but doubtful. Who else would you want in there in the seventh game of the World Series with the score tied in the ninth inning? Especially with the afternoon starting to turn gray.

The innings rolled on, the score remained tied. But it wasn't easy for Walter, who was in and out of hot water throughout the four innings he worked but who shot his way out with strikeouts.

It was still 3–3 in the bottom of the 12th, daylight was fading, and in the universe of baseball they were wondering if Walter Johnson would ever get his first World Series win. And then came a bit of luck, or, if your mind bends that way, some divine intervention, a reward for 18 years of virtuous service.

With one out, Washington's Muddy Ruel lifted a pop foul behind the plate. Moving toward what seemed an easy out, Giants catcher Hank Gowdy stumbled over his discarded mask, and the ball dropped. Ruel then doubled. Walter,

batting for himself, grounded to shortstop Travis Jackson, who fumbled, allowing Walter to reach first, with Ruel holding second. Earl McNeely then hit a grounder toward third baseman Freddie Lindstrom, but the ball struck something and took a bounding leap over Lindstrom's head. Home came Ruel with the winning run, and Walter was a World Series winner.

Losing pitcher Jack Bentley summed it up after the game when he said, "Walter Johnson is such a lovable character that the Good Lord didn't want to see him get beat again." It sure seemed that way.

Washington won the pennant again in 1925, sending Walter back into the Series. This time he reversed the pattern, winning his first two starts but losing the seventh game to Pittsburgh, 9–7, the Pirates raking him for 15 hits, with Harris—surely the sentimentalist this time—letting him go all the way.

Johnson pitched in the bigs until 1927, going 5–6 in his 21st and final year. He retired with a lifetime 416–279 record (most wins by a twentieth-century pitcher), his 110 shutouts, and 3,508 strikeouts. The latter was a hallowed major-league record that stood for more than half a century but was eventually surpassed by Nolan Ryan, Steve Carlton, Gaylord Perry, and Tom Seaver.

Walter came back to manage the Senators from 1929 through 1932 and did fairly well, with three first-division finishes in four years. He managed Cleveland for a couple of years, then left baseball.

Johnson died in Washington on December 10, 1946, a month after his fifty-ninth birthday, leaving behind a name that will always be synonymous with a speeding fast ball.

Alexander. "A deceptively easy sidearm motion."

GROVER CLEVELAND ALEXANDER

For years they sounded like some oak-and-leather law firm—Mathewson, Johnson, and Alexander. They were a triumvirate so sonorous to the ear and lordly to the imagination that they seemed among the noble bedrock of the republic. That is, if you were a baseball fan of a certain age, when their names and the resonance of their achievements were still fresh and crisp, before they were raised to pedestals.

They were, of course, Christy Mathewson, Walter Johnson, and Grover Cleveland Alexander, and they were the three greatest pitchers that ever lived—and no arguments (the same way that Cobb, Ruth, and Speaker were the outfield). The names, if you paid attention, were always recited in that same sequence: Mathewson, Johnson, and Alexander, as though implicit in the order of mention was their ranking in the pitchers' pantheon. Contemporaries generally felt that Mathewson was the greatest of the three, Johnson next, Alexander third. Naturally, there were dissenters, mostly from Amer-ican League partisans, who felt Walter was being slighted.

Well then, which of the three was truly the greatest? The answer is, With talents so sublime and records so dazzling, select any one of them and you will not be wrong.

Saint Paul, Nebraska, in the latter decades of the nineteenth century, was a town of some 2,000 people, center of an extensive farming area that was part of an endless, virtually treeless central Nebraska landscape, lonely and wind-blown, with soaring and spectacular skies. It was home and seedbed to the youngster who would grow up to glory amid cheering thousands in the great stadiums of baseball America.

Named for a sitting President of the United States (and later portrayed on the screen by a future president, Ronald Reagan, in *The Winning Team*), Alexander was born in St. Paul on February 26, 1887, growing up in the company of one sister and six brothers, of whom he was the next to youngest. He was "a big, strapping boy, tall, rangy, and strong," who worked his father's farm and once husked 1,300 bushels of corn in 13 days, which, someone said, "is pretty near a record for these parts."

He began playing ball with neighborhood pickup teams, and a strong right arm led him to the mound. The big leagues, far to the east, seemed so remote to a Nebraska farmboy that as a youngster Alex never dreamed of playing there. Mathewson, Johnson, Cobb, and Wagner were but names that blew in with the wind, playing at heights too sublime even for a youngster soon to be their equal to dream of emulating.

He worked for the telephone company, digging postholes (curiously, the same work Walter Johnson had done in Weiser, Idaho, a few years earlier), playing ball on the side and gaining increasing renown as a pitcher. His sizable talent did not go unnoticed, and he was soon recommended to the Galesburg (Illinois) club in the Illinois–Missouri League, with whom he signed in 1909.

He was 15–8 with Galesburg when a midseason accident ended his year—and nearly his career and life, too. While running from first to second on a double-play grounder, he got in the way of the shortstop's peg to first and took the ball's full impact in the head. He was unconscious for the next 36 hours. When he recovered, he found to his dismay that his eyesight had been deranged by the blow. His vision was blurred, with everything appearing in multiples.

Since Alexander's reputation had been growing and inquiries had been made concerning his availability, the Galesburg club followed a not-uncommon business ethic and said nothing about their young ace's disability. So when the In-

Phillies rookie pitcher Grover Cleveland Alexander in 1911

dianapolis club of the American Association put in a bid to buy him, Alex, still seeing everything in twos and threes, headed for Indiana. When he arrived and the ball club realized they had been taken, they sent the young man home. During the winter, Indianapolis, following a loose reading of the Golden Rule, did unto others what had been done unto them and sold Alex to Syracuse, then a member of the New York State League.

What the canny pirates in Indianapolis did not know, however, was that Alexander's vision had been restored to normal over the winter and that in the spring of 1910 the twenty-two-year-old right-hander was poised at the threshold of greatness.

Alexander was 29–14 with Syracuse in 1910, including one stretch where he allowed just one unearned run over 87 innings—the equivalent of nearly 10 consecutive shutouts.

The Phillies purchased Alex from Syracuse, and in 1911 the quiet, good-natured, freckle-faced Nebraska farm boy put together the most resounding rookie season ever by a pitcher. His won-lost record was a remarkable 28–13, he struck out 227 (a league record for a rookie until Dwight Gooden broke it in 1984), and pitched a league-high seven shutouts.

A year later he dipped to 19–17 but led in strikeouts with 195, the first of five times he achieved this. In 1913 he was 22–8 and again led in shutouts, with nine. Alexander's shutout totals are among his most eye-catching statistics—12 in 1915, a major-league single-season record 16 in 1916, and eight more in 1917, his last year in Philadelphia. (His 90 career blankers are second only to Walter Johnson's 110.) By themselves these totals are impressive, but when one considers that he was

He described himself as "a farmer, no more, no less." But he also pitched a little.

pitching in a hitter's haven, Philadelphia's cramped Baker Bowl, it makes his precision pitching impressive to the extreme.

After a 27–15 record in 1914, Alex launched a three-year span that elevated him to baseball's most rarefied precincts, alongside Mathewson and Johnson. These were his three successive 30-game seasons (equaling what Mathewson had done in 1903–05): 31–10, 33–12, 30–13, accompanied by league-leading earned run averages of 1.22, 1.55, and 1.83 and averaging 384 innings a season.

In 1915, a year in which he threw four

Starting pitchers for the first game of the 1915 World Series, Boston's Ernie Shore *(left)* and Alexander

one-hitters, he pitched the Phillies into the World Series, in which he split two decisions with the Red Sox. In 1916 and again in 1917, he pitched and won two games in one day.

By the end of 1917 he was, inevitably, Alexander the Great, and like his historical namesake had run out of worlds to conquer. He had replaced the recently retired Mathewson at the pinnacle of National League pitchers, even giving legitimacy to the once-unthinkable question: Was he better than Matty? There were those who said no, but many of them had begun with the premise that no one could ever be better than Mathewson. In trying to resolve the irresolvable, one must take into account the superior teams that Mathewson had behind him as well as the Mathewson mystique, enhanced by his personal stature, the almost-regal aloofness that made him an aristocrat among ballplayers. Mathewson, like DiMaggio decades later, was as close to a sublime one-man caste as baseball has to offer.

Alexander, on the other hand, was an unblended Nebraska farm boy, without the Mathewson grace or the Johnson aura of rugged homespun strength and humility. He was a quiet, pleasant-natured man who, apparently unawed by his phenomenal success, described himself as "a farmer, no more, no less." He opted for the simple pleasures, returning to St. Paul in the off season and hunting with his cronies in the cottonwood groves of the nearby Loup River, operating a small poolroom in town, and spending time with his many siblings.

Also, his arsenal lacked an identifying caliber weapon. Mathewson had his mysterious "fade away," Johnson his mind-numbing speed. But Alex was a man of the basics: fast balls and curves (he did throw an occasional screwball or fadeaway), all delivered with exquisite control, all delivered with a deceptively easy sidearm motion. "He looked like he was hardly working at all," one teammate said. "Like he was standing out there throwing batting practice."

"I consider my curve ball my main strong point," Alex told an interviewer. "I have pretty good speed and a good change of pace, which is important; but the main thing with me is curves." The plural usage is telling, for it was said that Alex could make the ball break anywhere from a few inches on out, and throw them all for strikes. Along with this assortment of breakers, his fast ball, which he modestly said was "pretty

Bill Killefer, Alex's favorite catcher

Alexander on the troopship heading for France in 1918

good," was considered second to none in the league. (Burleigh Grimes described it as "kicking in about three inches on a right-handed batter.")

Phillies manager Pat Moran had this to say about his ace: "There is nothing swell-headed about Alec, as there is about some stars. He is on an equality with the other players and always pulling for the team to win, whether he is pitching or not. Off the diamond Alec is just as friendly and sociable as he is during the game. His popularity as a player does not outweigh his popularity as a man."

In November 1917, Alexander and Bill Killefer (his favorite catcher) were dealt to the Chicago Cubs. Why were the Phillies willing to trade a man coming off

three consecutive 30-game seasons? Well, the nation had gone to war the previous April and the club was afraid their ace would soon be going into the military. They were correct. Alex appeared in just three games for the Cubs in 1918 before entering the army.

By July 11 he was in France, a member of the 342d Field Artillery of the 89th Division. He spent seven weeks at the front, much of it in heavy, mind-bruising combat.

The big guns had a nine-mile range and were capable of being fired four times a minute, dispatching 95-pound shells. With sound-deadening bits of cotton stuffed into his ears to muffle the thunderous explosions, Grover Cleveland Alexander fought his war, pouring shells into the distance and crouching prayerfully as the incoming charges roared and whistled and jarred the earth

With the Cubs in 1925

St. Louis Cardinals right-hander Grover Cleveland Alexander

around him. On more than one occasion, some far-off German gunner came close to blowing up a 30-game winner.

When he returned home after the armistice, Alexander was a changed man. Where he had been quiet before, now he was withdrawn, and when he smiled, a teammate recalled, "there was a sadness in it."

Several years before, in a laudatory article, he had been described as a man without vices, specifically a man who did not drink. When it began, or precisely why, no one knew, but he had begun to drift into alcoholism. There were also occasional fits of epilepsy (though none ever occurred on the mound). Something inside him had shattered; it would never piece itself together again.

He came back with a 16–11 record in 1919, a dull year for Grover Cleveland Alexander but brightened by 9 shutouts and a 1.72 ERA, both good enough to lead the league. A year later he was 27–14 for the Cubs, the sixth time he had won 27 or more, leading with 173 strikeouts and 1.91 ERA.

After two indifferent seasons in 1921 and 1922, Alexander came back in 1923 with a 22–12 record, pitching 305 innings and walking an incredibly low 30 batters, fewer than one every 10 innings.

By now he seemed irretrievably alcoholic, a loner who disappeared after a game to go and sit in some out-of-the-way speakeasy or maybe alone in his hotel room and try with Prohibition whisky to exorcise whatever demons were plaguing him.

"We left him alone," said Les Bell, a teammate of the later years. "And that's how he preferred it. He was a very kind and gentle man, and there wasn't a man on the team who didn't worship Grover Cleveland Alexander. But he just wanted to be by himself and drink. We never knew exactly why but guessed that it had something to do with the war. We heard he'd gone through some very bad times in France."

He was aging before his time, his perspective on things growing increasingly melancholy. He gave an interview in the early 1920s that had a sad, wistful quality about it.

"They say as a man grows old he begins to look back rather than forward," he said. "While I may not be old in years, I am old as a ball player, and with the major part of my career behind me, it is naturally pleasanter for me to look back on what has been than to look forward to what will be." He confided that he had once dreamed of equaling Cy Young's record of 511 lifetime victories but that the war had not only deprived him of a prime year but had also drained a good deal of his strength and stamina. He lamented also his lost opportunity of winning 30 games four years in a row, noting that no pitcher in modern times had done so. He wished he could have pitched a perfect game. (Note how high an Olympian aspires: 500 wins, four 30-game seasons in a row, a perfect game.) However, even if he had accomplished all those things, they would today still be less than the sum of his greatest moment, and for Grover Cleveland Alexander, awash with nostalgia in the early 1920s, that moment was still to come.

When Joe McCarthy took over the Cubs in 1926 he decided that the heavy-drinking Alexander, though still a winning pitcher, was a bad influence on some of the younger players.

"I liked Alec," McCarthy said. "I liked him a lot. But he had to go."

So in midseason 1926, the thirty-nine-year-old pitcher was waived to the St. Louis Cardinals. Alex was 9–7 with the Cardinals and helped Rogers Hornsby's club bring St. Louis its first pennant in the twentieth century. (Hornsby, a teetotaler, chose to ignore Alex's excesses as long as Alex was ready to pitch.)

Tony Lazzeri

In the World Series the Cardinals were matched with the New York Yankees of Babe Ruth, Lou Gehrig, Earle Combs, Bob Meusel, Tony Lazzeri, Waite Hoyt, Herb Pennock, et al., a team one year away from being called the greatest of all time.

The Yankees, heavy favorites, won the opener. In game two, however, Alexander, in a World Series for the first time since 1915, evened things up with a 6–2, four-hit win. By the time game six came, it was Alex again tying the Series at three all with an easy 10–2 victory.

Having worked nine innings the day before, Alex was not expected to pitch in the seventh game, though he told Hornsby the night before he would be available for a short stint if needed. The need came in the seventh inning. The Cardinals were winning 3–2, the Yankees had the bases loaded, there were two out, and the hard-hitting rookie Tony Lazzeri was at bat. At this point Cardinal starter Jesse Haines had to leave the game with a blistered finger.

Hornsby waved toward the bullpen and in walked, very slowly, a lanky, freckle-faced living legend, about to apply the final bit of burnishing to that legend.

It was an overcast day in Yankee Stadium, with an entire season of baseball now poised in the balance. It was the veteran Alexander versus the tough young Lazzeri in a classic generational confrontation.

Like Babe Ruth's alleged called shot in the 1932 Series, this moment comes to us misted in tales many and improbable. They said Alex was drunk, that he was hung over, that he had been asleep in the bullpen. None of it true. It couldn't have been true, not the way he pitched. He threw Lazzeri curves that crackled through the gray October air like the end of a bullwhip, and Lazzeri, connecting only for a resounding foul, struck out. Alex then retired the Yankees in the eighth and ninth innings, and the Cardinals were champions.

It remains Alexander's most imperishable moment on a baseball field, baseball's most storied and dramatically perfect strikeout. It is the sculpture that stands atop Alexander's block of records.

Alex was 21–10 in 1927, then 16–19, then 9–8, and now the flowing sands were all but gone. He was forty-two years old, his drinking had continued unabated, he sometimes came to the park drunk or unsteady, and he would occasionally disappear for several days. The Cardinals let him go in 1929. He caught on with the Phillies in 1930, a wretched homecoming to the stage of his glory years. The old sidearm magic was long gone now, and after going 0–3 he was released. He left the big leagues with a lifetime 373–208 record, the same number of victories recorded by Mathewson. Statistically, at least, history could not decide who was better.

Alexander's post-major-league years were two decades of pathos. He traveled with a semipro team, the House of David, whose gimmick was bearded players (this in days when major-league players were not permitted even wispy mustaches). Then, unable anymore to retire even the semipros, he left the diamond forever, surfacing here and there in odd jobs, still drinking, still epileptic, a tall, gaunt, haunting legend, a ghostly hero from a world that now seemed so remote as to have been dreamed in that time before the Great War.

He reappeared in New York in the early 1940s as an attraction in a 42nd Street flea circus, where with quiet dignity he sat on

Alexander in July 1930, just after his release by the Phillies

a plain wooden chair and answered questions, mostly about the mysteriously undiminishing Lazzeri strikeout, the achievement that clung to him like the last leaf on a nobly old and wintry oak. Then he seemed to swirl away in the cyclonic years of the war.

He was back in St. Paul, Nebraska, in the late autumn of 1950, back where it had all begun for the once young, tall, strapping farm boy with the quiet manner and shy smile. But where once he had been the community's pride, now Alex was an old man to be avoided, a cadger of drinks in side-street saloons.

He was living in a rooming house, and there he died sometime on the night of November 4, 1950, his dirge the lost wailing of autumnal prairie winds, far from the cheers and the applause, far from the sunshine, far from the glory, far, far away, in time and in spirit.

It's May 19, 1925, at Ebbets Field, and Vance is receiving $1,000 in gold from writer Fred Lieb for having been voted the National League's Most Valuable Player in 1924.

DAZZY VANCE

It started in Red Cloud (Nebraska) in the Nebraska State League, and then a year later it was Superior (Nebraska) in the same league, and then Hastings (Nebraska) still in the same league, and continued on with St. Joseph (Missouri) in the Western League, Columbus (Missouri) in the American Association, Toledo in the American Association, Memphis in the Southern Association, Rochester in the International League, Sacramento in the Pacific Coast League, and New Orleans of the Southern Association. By this time it was 1921, and Dazzy Vance, the man who had followed this tortuous, nomadic route through the professional baseball leagues of America was thirty years old. He had received a few sips of heady major-league wine with Pittsburgh in 1915, with the Yankees later the same year, and with the Yankees again in 1918. During these brief visits to the top of the mountain he had gathered unto himself 33 innings of indifferent work and an 0–4 record. So, in 1922, when he reached the

big leagues again with the Brooklyn Dodgers, what were the odds of this wayfaring right-hander becoming one of the great pitchers in National League history?

Arthur Charles (Dazzy) Vance—in some record books he is Clarence Arthur—was born in Orient, Iowa, on March 4, 1891. The family moved to Hastings, Nebraska, when the boy was five years old; there he worked on his father's farm, gradually developing a strong 6'2", 200-pound frame. He had enormously long arms which were described as "flailing wildly" when he went into his windup. With a delivery that included a high kick and a terrific forward thrust of his body, he was a formidable figure on the mound as he fired in his "shoots" (fast balls) and hard, sweeping curve that his favorite catcher, Hank DeBerry, said "embarrassed" a lot of right-handed hitters. "On an overcast day," DeBerry said, Dazzy "was sometimes hard to catch. I was charged with a lot of short passed balls because I

Vance during his brief trial with the Yankees in 1918

couldn't get my glove up in time to catch his shoots. So you can imagine what it was like to try and hit him."

The famous nickname derived from the young Vance's mimicking of a local farmer who called any wondrous thing a "daisy," pronouncing it "dazzy." (When Vance joined the Dean brothers on the Cardinals at the tail end of his career it gave the club a trio of pitchers known as Dazzy, Dizzy, and Daffy. The club also had a Ripper, a Pepper, and a Ducky. Altogether, they were known as the Gashouse Gang.)

Nebraska may have been far from the glory diamonds of the major leagues, but nothing in America was, or is, ever very far from that robust entity baseball, which seems to spring from the native soil as sweetly and as inevitably as the green grass itself. The husky farm boy pitched for his high school team in Hastings and then for some town teams in the surrounding area.

Dazzy's fast ball whistled keenly across the flatlands of southern Nebraska, and in 1912, at the age of twenty-one, he turned professional, signing with the Red Cloud club. He was 11–15 that year, then 11–14 the following year with Superior. After a 17–4 record with Hastings through the first half of 1914, he was sold to St. Joseph, where he was 9–8, giving him an overall 26–12 record for the year.

In 1915, Vance pitched the bulk of the season with St. Joseph (with a 17–15 record) and had his brief peeps at the big time with the Pirates and Yankees.

In 1916, Vance suffered the arm injury that would delay his rise to the major leagues by five years. The injury derived from some hijinks: "Some kind friend had told me that I had the makings of a good boxer," Dazzy said, "and I wanted to believe him." While sparring with his brother, Vance "wrenched my arm in trying to give him a short jolt which didn't connect." A doctor told him the arm would need five years before it fully restored itself, an estimate that proved uncannily correct.

Sore arm or not, Vance went on pitching, with just enough on the ball to get through one mediocre minor-league season after another. (The Yankees had another brief look at him in 1918 and again said no.)

In 1920, he was with Memphis and New Orleans in the Southern Association, compiling a 16–17 record. A year later he was 21–11 for New Orleans, and now he had all his smoke back. The Brooklyn Dodgers bought him, and in 1922 Dazzy hit the big leagues to stay.

The thirty-one-year-old rookie was an immediate success, putting up an 18–12 record and leading the league with 134 strikeouts and tying for the lead with five shutouts. He was also a highly noticeable force on the mound, catching the eye of Grover Cleveland Alexander, who said, "That fellow Vance has more stuff on the ball than any other pitcher in the league."

In 1923 Dazzy was 18–15 and again the strikeout leader with 197. A year later he burst through to first-magnitude stardom, turning in a season of blazing success. In pitching the Dodgers to within 1½ games of the pennant—won by John McGraw's Giants—Vance posted a 28–6 record, at one point winning 15 in a row. He led in strikeouts for the third consecutive year, with a remarkable 262—remarkable because only one other pitcher in the league that year fanned over 86 (Dazzy's Brooklyn teammate Burleigh Grimes, who had 135). Vance also led in earned run average with 2.16, a most impressive figure in a league that batted a collective .283. (Only three other National League pitchers had ERAs under 3.00 that year.)

Vance was so overpowering in 1924 that when it came to selecting a Most Valuable Player, he was chosen over Rogers Hornsby, who that year batted .424, the highest average recorded in the twentieth century.

In 1925 Vance was 22–9, including a no-hitter against the Phillies on September 13. He was a 22-game winner again in 1928. High among his achievements are his seven successive strikeout titles, from his first big-league season through 1928, a dual league record—for most years leading in strikeouts and most consecutive years leading in strikeouts.

One indication of how hard Dazzy poured his fast one in is that between 1918 and 1935, an era that embraced the hardest hitting in National League history, only three times did any pitcher attain the 200 mark in strikeouts, and each time it was Vance—262 in 1924, 221 in 1925, and 200 in 1928.

Dazzy's curve was by all accounts lethal, but when in a jam he preferred his fast ball. "The most comforting thing I know of in the pinch," he said, "is to be able to shoot the ball over with a zip that will hop over the swinging bat for a third strike." He estimated that 85 percent of

Dazzy firing in to the Cubs' Hack Wilson

his deliveries were fast balls. He "zipped" over enough of them to earn, along with his seven strikeout titles, four years of leading in shutouts, and an overall 197–140 lifetime record, a huge number of victories for a man who didn't score his first until the age of thirty-one. Dazzy was amply rewarded; his $25,000 salary in 1929 made him the league's highest-paid pitcher.

Dazzy was one of the more colorful ornaments on a club that was known in the high-spiraling 1920s as "the Daffy Dodgers." Managed by the rotund, genial, sometimes absent-minded Wilbert Robinson, the team was noted for its occasionally unorthodox hilarities. The most celebrated of these was the Adventure of Three Men on Third Base, in which Dazzy was a starring character.

The man who drilled the base hit that put into motion baseball's most storied base-running fiasco was Brooklyn's top slugger, Babe Herman, remembered for his lusty hitting, chancy fielding, and galloping base-path style. The notorious mixup occurred within the tolerant confines of Brooklyn's Ebbets Field on August 15, 1926. It was the bottom of the seventh inning, the score was tied 1–1 (Brooklyn versus the Boston Braves), the bases were loaded (Chick Fewster on first, Vance on second, and DeBerry on third), and Herman at bat. Babe ripped one off the top of the right-field fence, and things began to happen. In Herman's own words, this is how it all unfolded:

It hit the fence so hard that it bounced back far enough for the second baseman, Doc Gautreau, to run out and retrieve it. He picks it up and fires it to the shortstop, Eddie Moore, who's covering second, just as I'm sliding in there. I'm safe. Now, I'm lying on the ground and I hear Gautreau yelling to Moore to throw the ball home. I look around and catch a glimpse of somebody stopping midway between third and home. I figure it's Fewster. Who else could it be? DeBerry had scored easily, and Vance had been on second, so I was sure he'd scored, too. It had to be Fewster.

Babe Herman

Team president and manager Wilbert Robinson watching his ace signing a contract at the team's Clearwater, Florida, training camp on March 18, 1929

I figured Fewster was going to be caught in a rundown between third and home and that while he was jockeying around I could make third. So as soon as Moore throws the ball home, I get up and light out for third, keeping an eye on that rundown. Then I go sliding into third, and by gosh, who's jumping into the air to get out of the way of my spikes but Chick Fewster. He comes down behind me and I look up to see the umpire scratching his head. "Hey, Babe," he says, "you're out for passing Fewster on the baseline." That was a little technical, but he was right.

At that moment, Vance comes running back to third, jumps on the bag with both feet and says, "Ha, ha, I'm safe." "Yeah, you big Airedale," I said to him, "and you're the only one who is." So I got up and started walking away. Fewster goes over, picks up his glove and gets ready to play second base.

But Fewster was not out, not until Gautreau took the ball from the third baseman and tagged him, meaning that Herman had doubled into a double play. But why had Vance stopped between third and home when he could have scored easily?

"I asked him that later," Herman said. "He said that when the ball was hit he had gone back to second to tag up. 'Tag up?' I asked him. 'On a ball that was a few feet from going out?' You know, about thirty years later Vance was talking to a gathering down in Florida and he finally told the story. 'Don't blame Herman,' he said. 'I was the guy who really screwed the thing up.'"

Vance remained with the Dodgers until 1933, when he was traded to the Cardinals, where he pitched mainly in relief, logging a 6–2 record. The following year he was sold to Cincinnati, who released him in June, whereupon the pennant-bound Cardinals re-signed him, enabling him to get into the World Series for the only time in his career. In the 1934 Series against the Tigers he pitched 1 ⅓ innings, fanning three.

At the age of forty-four, Dazzy returned to Brooklyn for the 1935 season, closing out his career with a 3–2 record.

Vance died in Homosassa, Florida, on February 16, 1961.

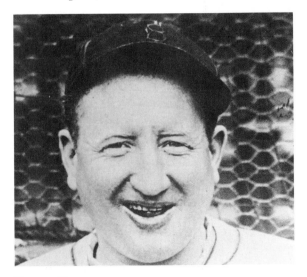

Dazzy Vance

Grove receiving the silver cup emblematic of having been voted the American League's Most Valuable Player in 1931

LEFTY GROVE

There are some record-book numbers that just don't look right, that seem like the creations of a dreamy youngster lying abed at night fantasizing upon what *he* would like to do in the big leagues. Babe Ruth's home-run totals fall into this category, as do Rogers Hornsby's batting averages and, if our young dreamer has set his conceits upon mound glory, Lefty Grove's won-lost records between 1927 and 1933. The latter read like this:

1927: 20–13
1928: 24–8
1929: 20–6
1930: 28–5
1931: 31–4
1932: 25–10
1933: 24–8

That's 172 wins against 54 losses over a seven-year span, or as near to being unbeatable as any major-league pitcher has ever been over so extended a period. Dur-

ing these flaming seven years the estimable Mr. Grove also led his league five times each in strikeouts and earned run average. Did all of this unprecedented and unequaled success make Mr. Grove happy? Well . . . not exactly.

Landmark pitchers like Christy Mathewson, Walter Johnson, and Grover Cleveland Alexander were temperate of disposition. Rube Waddell and Dizzy Dean were ebullient extroverts. Grove? The word *dour* was the one most used to connect with his persona. He was also moody, short-tempered, and, under the proper persuasion, volcanic. He was also extremely likable. It was all predicated on winning. He pitched, it was said, "with terrifying intensity," with an emotional investment not easily dissipated at game's end. To some he seemed an extremely complex man. Teammate Jimmy Dykes offered this appraisal: "Lefty was really a very shy person who always felt ill at ease and uncomfortable in the big cities and with a lot of people around. He

Robert Moses (Lefty) Grove in 1925

was basically a small-town guy, and all the crowds and hoopla made him tense and irritable. But give him a fishing rod and put him in a rowboat out in the middle of a quiet lake and he was the nicest guy in the world."

The small town that this nice, dour fellow came from was Lonaconing, Maryland, which lies in the narrow western area of the state. It was an area of rolling hills and soft-coal mines. There Robert Moses Grove was born, on March 6, 1900, one of four sons and three daughters of coal miner John Grove.

One by one the Grove sons joined their father underground, working the Georges Creek mines. Robert, however, felt a higher destiny calling him up from the nether world and back to the sunshine

and the green grass. He emerged on the wings of pure and indisputable logic: "I didn't put that coal in there, and I see no reason why I should have to take it out." He was around seventeen years old then.

Lefty evidently was not the born baseball junkie that so many others were; at age seventeen he hadn't played that much ball, and when he did play in the amateur games around town he was a first baseman. One day he took a relay from the right-fielder and from the edge of the outfield grass fired the ball home, a peg that his manager said came in so fast "I could hardly follow it with my eyes." After that, Lefty was a pitcher.

In 1920 he was pitching for Martinsburg (West Virginia) in the Blue Ridge League. He got into six games, running up a 3–3 record, but with 60 strikeouts in 59 innings. The lightning of his fast ball crackled like telegraph signals and reached the ears of Jack Dunn, owner of the Baltimore Orioles, then in the International League. Dunn, forever a part of baseball lore as the man who had sold Babe Ruth to the Red Sox six years earlier, took a hike up to Martinsburg, watched the tall (6'3"), sinewy young southpaw fire, and reached for his checkbook. Martinsburg accepted $3,500, and Dunn brought his second-greatest discovery back with him to Baltimore.

Lefty finished the season going 12–2 for the Orioles, and Dunn began entertaining offers for his prodigy. He entertained them for four years, waiting for the irresistible one. Over these four years Grove worked up won-lost records of 25–10, 18–8, 27–10, and 27–6, leading the league in strikeouts each year. Lefty never objected to remaining longer in the minors than he ordinarily would have. "Dunn treated us okay," he said, by

The greatest battery in baseball history, Grove *(left)* and catcher Mickey Cochrane.

which he meant he was drawing a salary higher than most major leaguers.

After the 1924 season, however, Connie Mack offered Dunn the grand sum of $100,600 for Lefty's contract (the extra $600 was tacked on in the name of history, to make it the largest minor-league transaction of all time), and Lefty joined the Philadelphia Athletics. Dunn had already turned down John McGraw's offer of $75,000, which suited Lefty just fine. "I wouldn't have wanted to play for McGraw, no sir," he said. Too bad, in a way; the fireworks displays between these two monumentally strong personalities would have provided baseball

lore with permanent animation.

So instead of serving under the sulfurous McGraw, Lefty went to work for Connie Mack, baseball's most conspicuous candidate for canonization. But even the gentle and patient Connie occasionally found himself tried to his utmost fiber by his short-tempered ace. One afternoon, Connie offered Lefty some quietly spoken words of advice after a particularly rough inning, only to be told to "go take a shit." Whereupon Lefty flung down his glove and seated himself in the corner of the dugout and seethed. Whereupon baseball's resident saint rose from his seat, walked the length of the dugout

Three of Connie Mack's aces. *Left to right:* George Earnshaw, Ed Rommel, and Grove.

in all his firmly erect dignity (while the rest of the players struggled to smother their laughter), confronted Lefty, and said sternly, "You go take a shit, Robert." For Connie, that was pure blasphemy, and even Grove pulled his cap down over his face and shook with laughter as the old man walked away.

Grove broke in in 1925 with a 10–12 record (his only sub-.500 season in 17 big-league years), but led the league with 116 strikeouts. He was to lead in whiffs his first seven years, equaling what Dazzy Vance was to do in his first seven years, beginning in 1922.

In 1926, Grove was 13–13, with his 2.51 earned run average leading the league, the first of a record-setting nine ERA titles he was to take.

In 1927 he was 20–13, launching a stretch of seven consecutive seasons of 20 wins or better. By now he was the left-handed terror of the American League, firing the fastest fast ball seen since the heyday of Walter Johnson, who bowed out that year. How fast was Grove? Precise measurements were not available in those days, but it is safe to assume that no mortal ever threw harder, righty or lefty, and certainly not over the course of nine innings.

"He could stand out there for a week

and barrel it in on you. I don't know where he got it all from." This is the testimony of Cleveland shortstop Joe Sewell, statistically the hardest man in baseball history to strike out. Sewell also offers a bit of baseball poetry in his description of the Grove fast ball at its mightiest: "Sometimes when the sun was out really bright he would throw that baseball in there and it looked like a flash of white sewing thread coming up at you." When asked what kind of action there was on a Grove swifty, Paul Richards replied, "There really wasn't any. It got there too fast to have time to do anything."

In 1929, Connie Mack's Athletics unseated the Ruth-Gehrig Yankees from atop the American League and ruled as champions for three straight years, winning the World Series in 1929 and 1930. Grove was 4–2 in his three World Series appearances.

"Really a very shy person . . ."

The heart of these mammoth Athletic teams was Al Simmons, Jimmie Foxx, Mickey Cochrane, and the pitching staff headed by Grove, which also included George Earnshaw and Rube Walberg. Across the three pennant years Lefty carved a composite 79–15 record.

On his way to his 31–4 record (and Most Valuable Player Award) in 1931, Lefty rang up 16 consecutive victories, tying the league mark for consecutive victories coheld by Smoky Joe Wood and Walter Johnson (both in 1912). With the chance to establish a new record, Lefty was beaten 1–0 by the St. Louis Browns, on a misplayed fly ball by left fielder Jim Moore.

That defeat provoked one of Grove's legendary explosions of temper. After the 1–0 loss had been sealed, ending his 16-game win streak, Lefty stormed into the clubhouse. Teammate Doc Cramer never forgot it:

The sparks were flying off Grove. Oh, I mean to tell you. I knew it was going to happen. Well, he was about three lockers down from me. I saw him stand up and take hold of the top of his shirt with both hands—we had buttons on our shirts in those days— stand like that for a second, and then *rrrip!* He tore that shirt apart so fast and so hard that I saw the buttons go flying past me, three lockers away. Then everything went flying—bats, balls, gloves, shoes, benches. He broke up a couple of chairs. He kicked in a couple of lockers. Nobody said a word. There was no point. You had to wait till the steam went out of him. Next day he was all right. But I never will forget those buttons flying past me.

One of Lefty's more notable victories occurred at Yankee Stadium on August 3,

Grove with the Red Sox in 1936

1933. The Yankees had gone 308 games without being shut out when Lefty faced them that day. Firing hard all afternoon, Grove ended that phenomenal streak, blanking the New Yorkers 7–0. He fanned six, getting Ruth three times and Gehrig twice, meaning that Lefty bore down when it mattered most.

On December 12, 1933, Mack, needing money in the deepening Depression, sent Grove and several other players to the Red Sox for $125,000.

A sore arm limited Grove to an 8–8 season; it also cost him the white-hot edge of his fast ball. Nevertheless, pitching with guile and cranking up the old blazer when he needed it, Lefty returned the next year to compile a 20–12 record, his eighth and final 20-game turnout.

Thereafter, he curve-balled his way to winning seasons of 17–12, 17–9, 14–4, 15–4, 7–6, and finally 7–7 in 1941, his last year. Pitching with what Ted Williams later called "the most beautifully coordinated motion I ever saw," a fading Grove was still good enough to win his last four ERA titles.

His seventh win in 1941, on July 26 against the Cleveland Indians, was Lefty's 300th, the figure he retired with, joining Mathewson, Johnson, Alexander, and Plank as the century's only 300-game winners. His record of 300–141 figures out to a .680 winning percentage, second only to Whitey Ford (.690) among twentieth-century pitchers.

Grove died on May 23, 1975.

Grove after victory number 300 in 1941

Carl Hubbell

CARL HUBBELL

The most exquisite display of pitching decorum in baseball history was turned in by one of the game's most modest and retiring heroes. The nature of this particular feat evokes images of blazing fast balls, a flamboyant style, muscular heroics. But in this instance there were no such fast balls, no flamboyance, no exhibition of great strength. It was done with tantalizing precision deliveries, and precise they had to be, for Carl Hubbell was staring directly into the mouths of five of the most explosive cannons in baseball.

It was a gray, muggy July 10, 1934, in New York City. The second annual All-Star Game was being played at Hubbell's home field, the Polo Grounds, and the New York Giants' left-hander was starting for the National League.

Establishing dramatic resonance for what was to come, the first two American League batters reached base, Detroit's Charlie Gehringer on a single and Washington's Heinie Manush on a walk. That left Hubbell in simmering water indeed, for the next three batters were Babe Ruth, Lou Gehrig, and Jimmie Foxx, three of the elite power hitters, not only of the day, but of all time.

Hubbell hoped to get Ruth to hit it on the ground—a sure double play with the thirty-eight-year-old Babe running. But Ruth never swung; he merely stood there looking "decidedly puzzled" as Hubbell, after wasting a fast ball, bent three uncannily thrown screwballs over the outside corner.

Lou Gehrig was next. The Yankee first baseman was in his prime, at that moment probably baseball's premier buster. Unlike Ruth, Lou had his rips, swinging futilely at Hubbell's smartly twisting screwballs. Gehringer and Manush executed a double steal on the third strike, but it was not to matter.

Jimmie Foxx, the Philadelphia Athletics' slugger—known as "the right-handed Babe Ruth" (that tells you something)—was the first righty to face Hub-

71

Ty Cobb: "Forget the screwball."

bell, but it made no difference. Jimmie stirred the muggy air with some mighty swings and the inning was over. Hubbell left the mound to an ovation from the nearly 50,000 customers.

But King Carl was not through. In the top of the second he struck out the first two batters he faced. The first was Chicago's Al Simmons, a right-hander of sublime achievement (he went into that season with a 10-year major-league batting average of .355). But Al went down swinging, as did the next man, Washington's hard-hitting Joe Cronin.

Five of baseball's greatest hitters in a row, and not a murmur from home plate. The Yankees' Bill Dickey finally broke the spell with a single. ("I was happy to see that," the laconic Gehringer said later. "It was starting to get embarrassing.") Hub-

bell then fanned Yankee pitcher Lefty Gomez.

Carl Hubbell's pitching in the 1934 All-Star Game, intertwined with the names of Ruth, Gehrig, Foxx, Simmons, and Cronin, has become one of baseball's enduring stories. Like a tale of the holiday season, it is renewed and told over again at All-Star Game time, a tale of a lone, lanky, sober-faced man armed only with a pitch eccentric in behavior and name, striking out in succession five of the game's noblemen. The tale, stirring in its compactness and purity, has come to delineate a career that was studded with other brilliant achievements, of greater and more majestic breadth. And, ironically, because of that very pitch, that quirky screwball, it was almost a career that never was.

Hubbell was born in Carthage, Missouri, on June 22, 1903. When the boy was four years old, the family moved to Meeker, Oklahoma, where he grew up on a pecan farm, and grew up to love baseball.

There is something telltale about the Hubbell personality in the story of his youthful affection for baseball. He loved to play the game, Hubbell recalled years later, but by his own admission did not at an early age begin nurturing visions of a big-league career. Perhaps to this innately shy and modest man the game was not meant for fame and glory and money, only for pure pleasure and clear enjoyment. Carl Hubbell, who became one of the radiant pitchers of all of baseball, began playing the game because he thought it was the finest thing a boy could do, an activity too innocent to have anything to do with ambition.

Nevertheless, talent is talent, and by 1923 he was signed with the Cushing club

A couple of left-handers rubbing shoulders at the 1933 All-Star Game, Carl Hubbell *(left)* and Lefty Grove

Carl Hubbell at work in the mid-1930s

of the Oklahoma State League. In 1925 he was pitching for Oklahoma City in the Western League, putting up a 17–13 record.

The twenty-two-year-old left-hander was already throwing the screwball, though not yet with the sureness for which he would become famous. For the uninitiated, the screwball is thrown with a reverse snap of the wrist. When thrown by a left-hander to a left-handed batter, it breaks down and in; to a right-hand batter it breaks down and away. According to Hubbell, it was not so much the ball's unorthodox flight that vexed the hitter as it was its reduced speed. "The trick," he said, "is to throw it over the top with exactly the same motion you use on a fast ball." In effect, Hubbell used his famous pitch as a changeup. His pattern was to set up hitters with fast balls and curves—which he threw adequately—and then get them out with screwballs, which he estimated he threw about 50 percent of the time.

In his prime he had such mastery over his screwball that occasionally he would deliberately fall behind 2–0 on a batter, knowing the man would be hitting, and then breaking off one of his reverse twisters that almost invariably was beat into the ground. "I did that for years," he said wryly, "and they never seemed to catch on."

After the 1925 season, Hubbell was sold to the Detroit Tigers. The young man who had never dreamed about playing in the big leagues reported to the Detroit spring-training camp in 1926. Almost immediately he received a disheartening command from Tiger manager, Tyrus Raymond Cobb himself: Forget the screwball. Cobb was of the conviction that the pitch, seldom seen in those years, could injure a man's arm. (Cobb was correct; it could hurt a pitcher's arm, and it finally hurt Hubbell's—a dozen years later.)

"There was nothing I could do about it," Hubbell said, adding succinctly, "After all, Ty Cobb was Ty Cobb."

Deprived of his money pitch, Hubbell impressed no one in the Tiger camp and was shipped to Toronto of the International League, with the order still standing: No screwball.

With a fast ball and curve of only average distinction, Hubbell needed his corkscrew delivery. Without it, he was 7–7 at Toronto. The following year the Tigers sank him lower in the minors, sending him to the Decauter (Illinois) club of the Three-I League. He was 14–7 there, but Detroit was no longer interested. The Tigers released him outright to Beaumont of the Texas League, and there began the swift turnaround in Hubbell's fortunes. The Beaumont skipper told him to "pitch the way you're most comfortable," and for Hubbell this meant a return to the screwball.

At midseason Hubbell was 12–9 and getting better. How Hubbell became a New York Giant is a story involving the Democratic National Convention, convening in Houston that year to nominate Alfred E. Smith as its presidential candidate. One of the delegates was Dick Kinsella, who also happened to be a scout for the Giants.

Bored with the proceedings, Kinsella slipped out of the convention hall and opted for that stimulating old American tonic, a ball game. Beaumont was in town, and their starter that day was Carl Hubbell. Kinsella sat enthralled as the poker-faced southpaw delivered a 1–0 victory. Kinsella headed back to his hotel

and contacted Giants manager John McGraw. McGraw liked what he heard, and in a short time a deal was cut—the Giants sent the Beaumont club a check for $30,000, and Beaumont sent the Giants Carl Hubbell.

Joining the Giants in July 1928, Hubbell broke in with a creditable 10–6 record. McGraw, aging irascibly, tyranically, even at times irrationally, was taken with the new man's aura of quiet, serious professionalism.

"He was very kind to me," Hubbell recalled years later. "I was young, and when I needed understanding, he gave it to me."

Placid, imperturbable, but at the same time fastidiously competitive, Hubbell went about his work with an unruffled demeanor that seemed more sublime than self-confident. McGraw's successor, Bill Terry, who took over in midseason

Hubbell (left) with Giants catcher Gus Mancuso

Hubbell in 1939

1932, said of his ace, "The tougher things got out there, the better he became. No fuss, no noise; he just worked like a machine."

In his second year, 1929, Hubbell was 18–11, including a no-hitter against the Pittsburgh Pirates on May 8 (the first no-hitter in the National League in nearly four years). He went on to pitch with solid efficiency over the next few years, with records of 17–12, 14–12, and 18–11.

In 1933 the Giants' left-hander rose from ace to master, beginning a run of five seasons in which he etched his name among the finest pitchers of all time. From 1933 through 1937 his won-lost records were 23–12, 21–12, 23–12, 26–6, and 22–8. He led in wins in 1933, 1936, and 1937; in earned run average in 1933 (1.66), 1934 (2.30), and 1936 (2.31); and shutouts in 1933 (10). He was the National League's Most Valuable Player in 1933 and 1936, and even more than his colorful contemporary Dizzy Dean (whom he beat in 8 of 11 matchups), its most intriguing pitcher. Chicago Cubs second baseman Billy Herman remembers the aura of Carl Hubbell:

When he was pitching, you hardly ever saw the opposing team sitting back in the dugout; they were all up on the top step, watching him operate. He was a marvel to watch, with that screwball, fast ball, curve, screwball again, changes of speed, control. He didn't have really overpowering stuff, but he was an absolute master of what he did have, and he got every last ounce out of his abilities. I never saw another pitcher who could so fascinate the opposition the way Hubbell did.

Hubbell helped pitch the Giants to pennants in 1933, 1936, and 1937. In the '33 Series against the Washington Senators he was 2–0, with no earned runs allowed in 20 innings. Overall, his World Series record is 4–2, with a 1.79 ERA for 50 innings of work.

History, with its keenly selective eye, will no doubt choose to remember Hubbell principally for his electrifying strikeouts in the 1934 All-Star Game; but the fact is, in the mid-1930s, by game and by season, he delivered a series of wondrous performances.

On July 2, 1933, he pitched an 18-inning 1–0 victory over the St. Louis Cardinals (Tex Carleton went the first 16 for the Cardinals) in which he allowed just six hits and no walks. Ten days later, on July 13, he began a string of consecutive scoreless innings that reached 46⅓ before it was stopped on August 1, establishing a National League record (later broken by Don Drysdale).

In 1936, when he was 26–6, he rang up 16 consecutive victories, from July 17 to the end of the season, and then began the next season with eight more before losing.

After 1937, the wear and tear of twisting away that screwball began to tell on Hubbell's arm, and though he pitched until 1943, he never again won more than 13 games in a season.

Hubbell left the active rolls with a 253–154 lifetime major-league record and a 2.98 earned run average. After retirement, King Carl took over as director of the New York (and later San Francisco) Giants' farm system, a job he remained in for more than three decades.

Dizzy striking a rather ceremonial pose for the photographer

DIZZY DEAN

About his bragging, Dean had this to say in a 1936 interview: "I've been accused of popping off a lot about myself. Maybe I do. People ask me questions and seem to want to hear me talk. I like to be accommodating. But as for bragging about my work, I don't look at it that way. There's plenty of things I can't do and I know it. I don't say anything about those things. But ever since I could hold a baseball, I thought I could pitch, and I think my record has proved it. Why shouldn't I say what I think?"

At times childishly temperamental, he would leave the team for several days, be suspended, return, be fined, reprimanded, battle with umpires, insult league president Ford Frick (who suspended him until Dizzy apologized), play practical jokes in hotel lobbies and on his manager, Frankie Frisch, hold out for more money, pout, sulk, and always return to the mound and in front of packed stadiums win and win and win.

In his heyday it was written of Dean:

His own teammates have been mad enough to club him, because of things he has said and things he has done. The general public has, at times, been disappointed to the verge of sheer disgust with Dizzy's ridiculous and foolish antics. But through it all he has battled blithely on, overcoming prejudice, wringing reluctant admiration from hostile crowds, winning out in the face of all opposition. As an example of a player with nerve and daring and matchless self-confidence, coupled with abilities of the highest order, Dizzy Dean has never had an equal. In all the annals of baseball he remains unique.

The country had fallen into the gray inertia of the worst economic depression in its history. The transition from the boisterously madcap, have-it-all twenties had been so ruthlessly sudden it left large segments of the country in utter shock, despair, and bewilderment.

There were few genuine gusts of laugh-

Dizzy Dean in 1930

ter and optimism in the 1930s, but one of them was the tall, lean, irrepressible former cotton picker from the unpaved country roads of Arkansas. He had a personality as fresh and zesty as a north wind, a smile that was wide and friendly, a noisy self-confidence that startled and delighted his dispirited countrymen, and, most important of all, a fast ball that crackled like heat lightning through the brutal monotony of Depression summers.

So here he came, in the midst of national despair, a quintessential hayseed brimming with exuberant joy and laughter, embodiment of rip-roaring rural verities that people thought had been crushed by the economy and blown away in dust-bowl storms. "You looked at him and you listened to him," one writer said, "and came away with the feeling that every-

thing was going to be all right." He soon became—along with that magical nickname—one of the most publicized men in America, a cornpone philosopher with a blazing fast ball and magnetic personality, and in the wake of a fading Babe Ruth the biggest drawing card in baseball.

Teammate Johnny Mize once described Dean's style on the mound, a description that embraced not only Dizzy the pitcher but Dizzy the man as well, the shrewd, self-proclaimed hayseed. "His reputation was as a fast-ball pitcher," Mize said, "and he was plenty fast. But he also knew how to pitch. He could throw you off with slow curves as well as anybody. He was a very deceptive fellow."

Deceptive indeed. A born showman, a wily observer of people, a journalist's delight. Born dirt poor, he put to use every advantage he had—wit, charm, spirit, and that fast ball (along with a big, sweeping curve that he called "my crooky"), which he delivered with a tireless right arm that flashed from an easy, fluid, long-striding motion.

There was no good reason for Dean's frisky disposition, not when you look at his hardscrabble upbringing. He was born Jay Hanna Dean in Lucas, Arkansas, on January 16, 1911, though from time to time he would announce a different name ("Jay Herman" was one of them) and different dates and places of birth "to give them reporters different scoops," he explained. It sounded ingenuous, but it was all part of the tune the mischievous country boy played at the expense of the city slickers.

Dean's mother died when he was very young. After a few years of elementary school, the future pitcher and his father and brothers earned their living chopping and picking cotton, rolling across

Dizzy letting one go

the red clay roads of rural Arkansas in the family jalopy, and into Texas and Oklahoma, looking for work in the fields, and when they got it, working long days in the broiling sun. There was nothing soft or easy or comfortable in this boy's childhood, and in later years it was all hidden behind that wide grin and consigned to private memories.

In 1927 he lied about his age and joined the army, serving with the field artillery at Fort Sam Houston in Texas, where, it is said, he was anointed with the famous nickname by a bemused sergeant, for what hijinks one can only imagine. But the discipline of army life was not for this soaring spirit, and Dean's father soon bought him out, a not-uncommon practice in those days.

On leaving the army, Dean found employment with the San Antonio Public Service Company, most noticeably on the company baseball team. Spotted by a Cardinals scout, he was signed to a contract.

In those years the country was abundantly stocked from sea to shining sea with minor leagues, and it was not unusual for a player to spend five or six years working his way through the thickets to the major leagues. But not the nineteen-year-old Dean. Everything about this American original was meteoric, rise and fall included. In 1930 he split the season between St. Joseph (Missouri) in the Western Association and Houston in the Texas League, combining for a 25–10 record. It earned him a brief trip to the top at the end of the season. He started one game for the Cardinals and delivered a three-hit victory.

The following spring he went to the

Dizzy *(right)* and brother Paul

Cardinals camp convinced he was a big leaguer. He probably was, too; but he was a bit too breezy about it all. He slept late, was noticeably casual in his work habits, popped off to his manager, Gabby Street, and earned himself a ticket back to Houston. He burned up the Texas League in 1931 with a 26–10 record, and now there was no stopping him.

Dean joined the Cardinals in 1932 and was an immediate success, going 18–15 and leading the league in strikeouts with 191. A year later the Gashouse Gang was forming, a raucous, colorful, hard-playing band of marauders who had Frankie Frisch as their manager and Dizzy as their most vivid personality. They also included outfielder Joe Medwick, third baseman Pepper Martin, shortstop Leo Durocher, first baseman Ripper Collins, and soon Dizzy's brother Paul, known as "Daffy" but who was actually the antithesis of his big brother, being a reticent young man who could fire the ball extremely hard.

In 1933 Dizzy posted a 20–18 record, again leading in strikeouts, with 199. On July 30 he set a one-game strikeout record by fanning 17 Cubs. He was by now cajoling the writers to refer to him as "the Great One" and was predicting his shutouts. When told that this was immodest,

he said, "If you say you're gonna do it, and do it, it ain't braggin'."

The following year was a memorable one for Dean and for the Gashouse Gang. Dizzy achieved the record books with a season that was almost gem perfect, posting a 30–7 won-lost record, and he remains the only National League pitcher since Grover Cleveland Alexander in 1917 to win 30. No matter how buoyant his spirits and lovable his personality, it is those 30 wins in 1934 that make Dizzy Dean stand out on a relief map of baseball.

He started 33 times that year and completed 24 games. He also relieved 17 times, a remarkable figure for an ace pitcher but typical for Dean, who frequently badgered Frisch into letting him go down to the bullpen. (He averaged 15 relief appearances per year between 1932 and 1936.) Dean, who led the league in strikeouts for the third straight time, with 195, and in shutouts with 7, won 4 of his 30 games as a relief pitcher.

With brother Paul joining the team that year, Dizzy boasted that they would win 45 between them. He was wrong—they won 49, with Paul winning 19 as a rookie (he would do the same the next year, and then his arm went dead).

The season was not without its controversy. In mid-August Dizzy insisted that Paul, who was earning $3,000, be given a raise. The club refused, whereupon the brothers threatened to strike, which they did briefly. When that was settled, Dizzy was fined and suspended for failing to appear for an exhibition game in Detroit and for shredding several uniforms in a fit of anger. It was all settled, of course, with the Deans paying their fines, with Dizzy paying for the uniforms, and then with the brothers going on to pitch the Cardinals to the pennant in the waning days of the season.

In the World Series against Detroit, the script went according to Dizzy's prediction: "Me and Paul are gonna win four." They did, each winning two, with Dizzy throwing an 11–0 shutout against the Tigers in the seventh game.

By now Dizzy was baseball's number-one man, its greatest drawing card, and one of the most famous men in America, considered enough of a national resource in those heavy-hearted times to merit a finger-wagging editorial from the *Sporting News* warning him "not to forget his origins," an admonition prompted by Dizzy's yellow convertible and his wintering in Florida.

Dean remained a fresh-flowing fountain of joy and excitement for the next two years, with records of 28–12 and 24–13 in 1935 and 1936, giving him a total of 120 for

Two of America's most famous men posing as writers, Dean *(left)* and entertainer Al Jolson

his first five big-league seasons, an average of 24 per year.

More than likely he would have gone on at that pace: He was just twenty-five years old, and the Cardinal teams he was pitching for were getting better and better. At the All-Star break in 1937 he was 12–7, on the way to another big year, when he was brought down, first by an accident and then by his own impetuousness.

Dizzy started the game for the National League in Washington, D.C., and had worked his way to two out in the bottom of the third inning. The batter was Cleveland's Earl Averill. Averill lined a low, sizzling smash through the box. Dean did not have time to either stop the ball or get out of the way, and it smashed into the big toe of his left foot. The toe was broken, and it soon became to Dizzy as a heel had been to Achilles.

Cautioned not to return to the mound until the digit was fully healed, Dizzy could not wait. Returning to the mound prematurely, he began favoring the still-painful toe by throwing with an unnatural stride and delivery. Pitching in Boston against the Braves, he felt something

Dizzy and Detroit's Schoolboy Rowe during the 1934 World Series

Dean *(right)* and Yankee rookie Joe DiMaggio at the 1936 All-Star Game

suddenly pop in his right arm. And just like that—like a piece of elastic that snaps and remains forever limp—the magical right arm of Dizzy Dean became like the arms of millions of other men, blessed with every function and capability except whistling a baseball past big-league hitters.

The career of Dizzy Dean was for all intents and purposes over. He finished the 1937 season with a 13–10 record. The following spring he was dealt to the Cubs for several players and a huge amount of money for the time, $185,000. The Cubs had no illusions about him; they knew they were getting damaged goods, but the thought of possessing Dizzy Dean was so beguiling they went ahead with the transaction.

Using all his acquired pitching know-how, Dean slow-balled his way through a 7–1 season (fanning just 22 batters in 75 innings), helping the Cubs to the pennant.

Dean's final moment of glory came in the 1938 World Series against the hard-hitting New York Yankees. Skipper Gabby Hartnett started him in the second game, and Dizzy's slow curves and meticulous control kept the Yankee sluggers off balance. Going into the top of the eighth inning he was nurturing a 3–2 lead when the light-hitting Frankie Crosetti stunned him with a two-run homer. The Yankees went on to win, 6–3. Dizzy Dean's setting sun had thrown off one last ray of poignant glory.

He held on for another two years, pitching when his aching arm permitted, posting 6–4 and 3–3 records, and then he was gone. His lifetime major-league record reads 150–83, most of it accumulated during those five glorious years when he ran like a riptide through the still waters of

Twenty-seven years old, a broken career, and a strange uniform

America's darkest journey.

In the 1940s he began his second career as a broadcaster. Behind the microphone he was as garrulous and irreverent as ever, yelling from the booth at players and umpires, mangling the language with a virtuosity that may or may not have been calculated, and, as he had always done, in times good and bad, renewing the legend of Dizzy Dean.

Dean died on July 17, 1974, in Reno, Nevada.

Bob Feller: They said the ball got smaller as it came toward you.

BOB FELLER

In the days of the frontier, "fastest" referred to a gunslinger's hand, how quickly it could unholster his six-shooter and fire. They have become the romantic names of the Old West, remaining in bas-relief on the recession of history. As the gunfire began to drift away and the dusty main streets of myth and legend were forced to accept the respectability of paving blocks, "fastest" came to mean another brand of romanticized American—the man on the mound in the country's favorite game, most specifically the one who could fire the ball plateward with speed to stir the imagination. The great fast-ball pitchers were a breed apart, uniquely gifted, kings of the hill, and, like their more lethal precursors in the realm of the "fastest," gripping in confrontation.

There had been Waddell and Johnson and Grove, and then in the 1930s there came to the major leagues a youngster, a teenager, to match any of the "fastest draws" who had gone before and any who would come later, a boy whose name was set in headline type virtually from the beginning.

There was something prototypically American about this boy Bob Feller. He was a dynamo of positive force rising abruptly from out of Depression doldrums, with a personality as fresh and direct as the fast balls he rocketed in from the mound. From the very beginning he was special, something different, and everyone knew it and stood back in awe and wonder. He was a prodigy in a game that was never made for them, and indeed had never had one. Not only was he blindingly fast, but it sounded as though he practiced black magic out there: "The ball looks smaller when he throws it," one batter said, "I swear." This went against all logic of speed and mass: Something that traveled *away* from you at great speed was what turned smaller to the eye, not an object that came *toward* you. The hand of Bob Feller, it seemed, delivered a baseball under different physical laws.

His story is American homespun at its purest. A product of the national heartland, he was born in Van Meter, Iowa, on November 3, 1918, son of an Iowan corn-

Main Street, Van Meter, Iowa, in the early 1930s

and-hog farmer, William Feller, who had a dream and an ambition that was high, wide, and handsome—a big-league career for his son.

William Feller first played ball with his son in the house, playing catch from the kitchen to the living room. Then it was outside, in the yard; and in the long, dead winter months it was in the barn two or three nights a week, under a primitive lighting system the farmer had rigged up. And even more: The corn-and-hog farmer fenced off a pasture, put up some chicken wire, built benches, a small grandstand, measured off a playing field, and declared it a ball park. (This was a dream of sweet innocence and gritty resolve both.)

Some of the neighboring farmers shook their heads and thought William Feller might be overdoing it a bit, that he might be instilling too many impractical ideas in the boy's head. But the corn-and-hog farmer paid no attention. This was, after all, his dream for his boy; and besides, he knew something those farmers didn't, because he was the one holding the catcher's mitt up to those pitches, seeing and feeling the boy's speed increase year by year.

"I could always throw hard," Bob Feller

said. "Even when I was eight or nine years old."

And he worked hard, too. It wasn't all baseball on that farm. Baseball came after the cow milking and the pig feeding and the barn cleaning and the fence building and all those other chores that built those powerful arms and shoulders and back.

At the age of sixteen his speed was ferocious. To hear the locals describe it, if he had fired his fast one through a row of those Iowa cornstalks he might have set the whole field afire. It was an umpire in American Legion ball, a most unimpeachable witness of the boy's speed, who alerted the Cleveland Indians to the phenomenon.

In the summer of 1935, a Cleveland scout, Cy Slapnicka, after taking his time about it (cometary sightings were not uncommon in the hyperbole that sometimes lit up the baseball firmament), finally showed up and stood among the alien corn. Slapnicka was forty-nine years old, a former big-league pitcher who had been up briefly with the Cubs in 1911 and Pirates in 1918. Thus he had been acquainted with Mathewson and Alexander, and one assumes that this baseball lifer had also seen Johnson and Grove. So one can further assume that Slapnicka believed he had seen what grandeur and alchemy might issue from a pitching mound.

And then he saw Bob Feller, and he must have felt like the man who discovered fire. He signed the boy to a contract (for a bonus of an autographed ball and $1), then returned to Cleveland to report to his employers that he had found "the greatest pitcher in history." From anyone, this was an astounding statement; from a man known to be cautious in his pronouncements, it was most astounding. And he may have been absolutely correct.

In 1936 the seventeen-year-old Feller was traveling with the Cleveland Indians, a nonroster player who worked out with the club every day. (The Indians felt he was still too green for big-league ball and were unwilling to trust him to the uncertain handling of a minor-league manager.)

During the break for the 1936 All-Star Game, the Indians had scheduled an ex-

It's August 12, 1940, and Feller has just notched his 20th win of the season. A few teammates (each of whom homered in the game) have gathered around. *Left to right:* First baseman Hal Trosky, Feller, outfielders Roy Weatherly and Beau Bell.

hibition game with the St. Louis Cardinals. The club decided to give the boy a bit of exposure to big-league hitters, limiting him to three innings.

So young Bob Feller took the mound. Was he nervous? "I was never nervous on a pitching mound," he said. The nerves, in fact, were twitching on the other side of the field. Reportedly, the Cardinals' playing manager Frankie Frisch took one look at the boy with the wide-swinging windup and big leg kick pop a fast ball and scratched himself from the lineup. Reportedly, when shortstop Leo Durocher faced the youngster, he took two strikes and walked away, telling the umpire he could have the other one. Reportedly, when Dizzy Dean—then the greatest pitcher in the corral—was asked by photographers after the game if he would pose with Feller, he replied, "Maybe you'd better ask *him* if he'll pose with *me*."

Instant lore, in other words, because in three innings against the swashbucklers

Feller *(right)* with batterymate Rollie Hemsley

One of baseball's classic confrontations, Feller versus DiMaggio. The date was April 30, 1946, and Feller is in the midst of no-hitting the Yankees at Yankee Stadium.

known as the Gashouse Gang the Iowa farm boy, beginning to fill in the contours of his father's grand dream, yielded just two hits and struck out *eight*.

The Indians quickly added the boy to the roster, and the 20 years of Robert William Andrew Feller had begun. If there had been skeptics after the Cardinals game, they were silenced after Feller's first big-league start, on August 23, 1936, against the St. Louis Browns. The boy turned in a spectacular performance, striking out 15. After the game umpire Red Ormsby, in the league since 1923, pronounced the boy faster than Johnson or Grove, which in the universe of baseball was as close to heresy as you could come.

On September 13, Feller did even better, striking out 17 Philadelphia Athletics, breaking Rube Waddell's old American League record by one and tying Dizzy Dean's major-league record. It hit the newspapers, Feller said, "like thunder and lightning, and I guess that's when people began to realize I was for real."

Feller was 5–3 that first year, with 76 strikeouts in 62 innings (in an era when strikeouts were much fewer than they are today). A year later, hampered by a sore arm, he was 9–7, with 150 strikeouts in 149 innings. Thirty-one American League pitchers had more innings pitched than Feller that year; only two had more strikeouts.

In 1938, still only nineteen years old, he was 17–11, taking the first of his seven strikeout titles with 240, including a record-setting 18 against the Tigers on October 2. It should also be noted that he set a major-league record that year with 208 bases on balls, meaning that the young man with the frightening speed and equally frightening curve ball had

Bob Feller

less than precision control. Facing Feller in those prehelmet days, a batter had to have survival as much as success on his mind. The youngster's stuff was so awesome that certain managers would flash the take sign to a particularly weak-hitting right-handed batter, not wanting their man to swing at what might be ball four, reasoning that if it was a strike he was not going to hit it anyway.

In 1938, Feller pitched the first of the 12 one-hit games of his career, by itself a remarkable statistic.

In 1939 he was in full bloom as the most spectacular and exciting pitcher in baseball. He was alone at the top, in achievement as well as in the national imagination, alone as Johnson had been, and Grove, and Dean, and later as Koufax would be: gifted, dominant, and original.

Bob is taking the subtle approach in contract negotiations with Cleveland owner Bill Veeck. The year is 1950.

He rang up a 24–9 record, leading in wins, strikeouts (246; only one other pitcher in the league, Bobo Newsom, with 192, had over 129), and complete games (24).

In 1940 he was even better. Mounting a 27–11 record, he began by pitching major-league baseball's first, and thus far only, opening-day no-hitter, against the Chicago White Sox on April 16. He led in wins, earned run average (2.62), strikeouts (261), shutouts (4), complete games (31), and innings (320).

A year later he was 25–13, leading in wins for the third year in a row, in strikeouts (260), shutouts (6), and innings (343).

And then it all went into long suspension. Disdaining the deferral he could have obtained as a farmer whose father was too ill to run the farm, Feller enlisted in the navy immediately after Pearl Harbor and went to war. Further disdaining the preferential treatment he could have had as a big-league star, he opted for combat duty, and he had plenty of it aboard the battleship *Alabama*, seeing action at Tarawa, Iwo Jima, and other blood-and-thunder Pacific outposts.

Feller did not return to baseball until late in the 1945 season, meaning he had missed almost four full—and prime—years, a gouging of major-league service that has helped feed the Feller myth and stirred the reveries of baseball romantics with the tantalizing question: What would his record look like with the missing years included? There are probably 1,000 strikeouts (at the least) unrecorded, meaning Feller would have been the man who broke Johnson's all-time mark; and probably 100 wins unrecorded, which would have elevated him to the most sublime statistical heights.

When the 1946 season began, there was some speculation about how much the now twenty-seven-year-old speedballer might have lost during the past four years (the few games he pitched in the '45 season were not considered significant because he had not had time to work himself back into shape; also, it wasn't until 1946 that all the top-line players were back from military service).

Feller answered the question early—he no-hit a bruising Yankee lineup on April 30—and kept answering it all summer long. He posted a 26–15 record and lead the league in everything there was to lead in: wins, strikeouts (348), shutouts (10), complete games (36), innings (371), and even in appearances (48). His strikeout total established a new major-league record, although later research showed that Rube Waddell had fanned 349 in 1904.

There were more solid seasons awaiting him, but 1946 was a peak that Feller never reached again. He won 20 in 1947 and 22 in 1951 and led in strikeouts in 1947 and 1948, but the years of supreme glory, as luminous as any in baseball history, were now behind him.

In 1948 Feller finally made it to the World Series, the Indians winning their first pennant since 1920. In the opening game he dueled brilliantly with Boston's Johnny Sain, coming away a 1–0 loser despite pitching a two-hitter. The run was controversial. It came in the last of the eighth. With Boston's Phil Masi on second base, Feller whirled and fired to shortstop (and manager) Lou Boudreau. Umpire Bill Stewart called Masi safe on an extremely close play, with many people feeling Masi was out. A moment later, Tommy Holmes laced a single to left, scoring Masi as the only run of the game. In a later appearance in the Series, Feller was hit hard.

On July 1, 1951, the man they called "Rapid Robert" fired his third no-hitter, against the Detroit Tigers.

The Indians won again in 1954, with an aging Feller, fourth on the staff now behind Bob Lemon, Early Wynn, and Mike Garcia, logging a 13–3 record. The Indians were swept in the World Series by the New York Giants, and Feller never had the chance to start.

How fast? "In all probability better than 100 miles an hour."

Rapid Robert about to fire

Cleveland player-manager Lou Boudreau *(left)* and Feller

Feller retired in 1956, closing out one of baseball's most pyrotechnic careers, his sensational displays of speed casting him among the game's few genuine legends.

How fast was he? In 1946 a photoelectric-cell device borrowed from the United States Army was set up at home plate at Washington's Griffith Stadium. Feller fired several dozen pitches through it and was clocked as high as 98.6 miles per hour. Feller claimed, and most hitters bore him out, that he generally threw faster and faster as a game progressed, maintaining his speed through nine innings. In his prime he in all probability threw better than 100 miles an hour. In addition, he snapped off a fast curve that some batters, particularly right-handers, said was even more potent and less hittable than his fast ball.

The Iowa farm boy retired with a 266–162 record, with those four haunting years missing. Slot those prime seasons into his accounts and it is likely he would have surpassed Mathewson and Alexander in victories and have been second only to Johnson among twentieth-century pitchers.

In 1935 Cy Slapnicka had come to Iowa and seen a sixteen-year-old boy deliver glorious fast balls and pronounced him "the greatest pitcher in history." The scout had not been far wrong, if at all.

Warren Spahn in 1942

WARREN SPAHN

Gene Conley, a fine right-handed pitcher who was a teammate of Warren Spahn's on the Milwaukee Braves in the 1950s, had this reminiscence of the gifted left-hander: "Spahn hated to miss a turn. He expected to pitch every fourth day no matter what. If your turn was rained out and he was due the next day, then you sat it out and he pitched. I remember one time it didn't work out that way and they started me and held Spahn back a day. He didn't like that at all. I heard he went up to the front office and got it squared away. He didn't want to miss a turn. And I'm not being critical of him; to the contrary, I think his attitude was great." Conley also said of Spahn, "He loved baseball and he loved to pitch; you got the feeling sometimes that pitching was his whole life."

Spahn maintained his great attitude not for a season or two but for a career of 21 years, 19 of them as a full-time starter. Between 1947 and 1963, he never started fewer than 32 games a season, and what he started he intended to complete: he led the National League in complete games nine times, including a record seven years in a row from 1957 through 1963 (he was forty-two years old in that last year).

Statistics. They are the story of Warren Spahn's professional life. His page in the record book glows and sparkles. Those splendid numbers can grow monotonous in their recital, for no pitcher in modern times was as uncannily consistent, at the highest levels of achievement, for so long. He won 20 games or better 13 times, a modern major-league record he shares with Christy Mathewson. Eight times he led in games won, another major-league record. His 63 shutouts are a National League record for left-handers, just one under Eddie Plank's major-league mark. He led in strikeouts four times, earned run average three times, shutouts three times. And the capstone of all his statistics—363 victories, putting him in second place in National League history, just 10 under the 373 won by both Mathewson and Alexander.

What is most impressive about those

Mainstays of the Boston Braves pitching staff in 1950. *Left to right:* Vern Bickford, Johnny Sain, Warren Spahn.

363 wins is that Spahn did not win his first big-league game until he was twenty-five years old.

This record-setting paragon of sterling consistency was born in Buffalo, New York, on April 23, 1921. (He was named for the man then in the White House, Warren Harding, whom he would eventually out-glory.)

The young southpaw compiled a scintillating record on the mound for Buf-

falo's South Park High School, where he was spotted by a scout for the Boston Braves, who eventually signed him to an $80-a-month contract.

Spahn started in 1940 with the Bradford (New York) club in the Pony League, where he broke in with a modest 5–4 record. A year later he was with Evansville (Indiana) in the Three-I League and was 19–6. This earned him a promotion to the Braves' spring-training camp. Manager

Casey Stengel kept the youngster with the big club for a few weeks into the season, letting Spahn mop up a few lost causes before sending him out to Hartford in the Eastern League. Spahn was 17–12 with Hartford and then went off to war.

He spent three years in the Army Corps of Engineers. When he returned to baseball after the war, those who had known him before commented on how he had matured, how "poised" he had become. There was reason for it. The future Hall of Famer had campaigned through Europe with the First Army, caught a piece of shrapnel in the neck, earned a battlefield commission during the Battle of the Bulge ("They were running out of officers," he said wryly), was nearly killed at Remagen Bridge, and came home with a Purple Heart and a Bronze Star. With these experiences behind him, clearly nothing that could occur on a ball field was going to intimidate him.

Not discharged until April 1946, Spahn went straight to Boston and began his big-league career in earnest. After slowly working himself back into shape, he won his first game on June 14, 1946.

After going 8–5 in 1946, he was 21–10 in

Spahn in 1946, back from the war

1947, leading in ERA (2.33) and shutouts (7). In 1948 his 15–12 record helped the Braves to their first pennant since 1914. He was 1–1 in the World Series against Cleveland.

Spahn began winning and simply never stopped. Between 1947 and 1963, he averaged 20 wins per season, racking them up year after year with almost programmatic regularity. Throughout these 17 years he never went more than one season without winning his 20, missing, in fact, only four times. His biggest winning seasons came in 1953 and 1963, when he rang up records of 23–7.

Part of Spahn's remarkable success can be attributed to his ability to adapt his style of pitching to the passing years, making mid-career adjustments that were virtually seamless. When some of the heat began cooling on his fast ball (plenty quick but never overpowering), he began cultivating the screwball, and then later on a more varied assortment of breaking pitches, all of which he delivered with expert control.

He was considered very much the cerebral performer. "Every pitch he throws has got an idea behind it," Braves pitching coach Whit Wyatt said of Spahn. (It was Wyatt, in 1958, who helped the then thirty-seven-year-old Spahn master the slider, adding yet another pitch to the left-hander's repertoire.) One of Spahn's great strengths on the mound, according to Wyatt, was his ability to throw slow curves and sliders for strikes when behind on the count.

Spahn's razor-sharp control made him a tough man to umpire. "He's always on the corners," one umpire said. "You get more close calls with him on the mound than any other five pitchers put together. Sometimes I feel like walking out there and telling him, 'Warren, the damned plate's seventeen inches wide.' "

But it was all part of Spahn's artistic design. "I never throw a ball down the middle of the plate," he said. "In fact, I ignore the twelve inches in the middle of it and concentrate on hitting the two and

"Superbly stylish in the demonstration of his art . . ."

a half inches on each side or corner of it."

On the mound he was the embodiment of style and grace. He kicked high with his right foot and followed with a long stride that rendered him smooth and flowing as he delivered. Throwing every pitch with the identical flawless motion made him hard to anticipate and hard to hit. As Ted Williams was at the plate, so was Spahn on the mound—superbly stylish in the demonstration of his art.

Spahn helped himself by developing what was regarded as the most deceptive pickoff motion to first base; also, his 35 lifetime home runs are a record for National League pitchers.

He just kept getting better and better. In 1956, at the age of thirty-five, he launched the first of six consecutive 20-game seasons, culminating with his 23–7 in 1963 at the age of forty-two. In 1957 he won the Cy Young Award, the same year he helped pitch the Braves to the first of two straight pennants. In his three World Series he was 4–3, including a two-hit shutout over the Yankees in 1958. On September 16, 1960, he pitched the first no-hitter of his career, stifling the Phillies. The following year, on April 28 (five days after his fortieth birthday), he delivered another no-hitter, against the Giants. After the game, the Giants' Willie Mays voiced the batter's traditional lament when discussing Spahn: "He keeps you off balance with changing speeds all day and never gives you a chance to get much bat on the ball."

The seemingly endless mileage began running out of Spahn's arm in 1964. He dropped from 23–7 to 6–13 and at the end of the season was sold to the New York Mets, where he was reunited with his first big-league manager, Casey Stengel. The Mets released him in midseason, and

Spahn caught on with the San Francisco Giants, with whom he ended his big-league career in 1965.

Spahn's skills and longevity produced

Spahn with the New York Mets in 1965

a 363–245 career record. His win total places him fourth among twentieth-century pitchers, behind the great trinity of the century's first quarter—Johnson, Mathewson, and Alexander. Spahn's 382 complete games rank him fifth among twentieth-century pitchers, with again the great trinity, plus Eddie Plank, ahead of him. In innings pitched, Spahn's 5,246 has him ranked third among this century's pitchers, trailing only Johnson and Gaylord Perry.

In 1964, just as Spahn's career began finally to sputter, Branch Rickey, on the scene for nearly 60 years, had this to say about him: "He is a consummate artist—a student and a scholar but also a polished craftsman. No pitcher ever has made such magnificent use of his God-given equipment. . . . He has no equal. He knows how to pitch, when to pitch, what to pitch. Others may not agree with me . . . but my honest opinion is that there never has been a better pitcher in the history of baseball than Warren Spahn."

Robin Roberts in action. It came from "within."

ROBIN ROBERTS

"Robin Roberts was one of the most efficient pitchers that ever lived," said Eddie Sawyer, who managed the Philadelphia Phillies during some of Roberts' heyday years with that team. "He completed many games with only 70 or 75 pitches. That's what I call efficient. He got the ball from the catcher and fired it right back in." And usually for strikes. From out of a low, gently rocking windup he fired fast ball after fast ball, right across the knees.

The man who broke many of Grover Cleveland Alexander's Philadelphia club records was a pitcher of remarkable stamina. For six successive years (1950–1955) he led the National League in games started, for five successive years (1952–1956) he led in complete games, and for five successive years (1951–1955) he led in innings pitched, with over 300 each year. Along with speed and stamina, the third hallmark of the pitcher Robin Roberts was his control: In 1952, he walked just 45 in 330 innings.

Roberts was born in Springfield, Illi-nois, on September 30, 1926, son of a Welsh miner who had emigrated after the First World War. Young Robin grew up loving baseball and playing it in the wide open spaces outside Springfield, where the family lived. His first baseball was a Bull Durham tobacco sack stuffed with grass and tied together with twine, his first bat a cricket stick his father had brought with him from Wales.

When he was nineteen years old, Roberts went to Michigan State on a basketball scholarship. He didn't try out for the baseball team until his sophomore year, and then it was as a third baseman. But when he heard the team needed pitchers, he decided he was a pitcher. They saw him throw and they agreed.

"I could always throw the ball hard," Roberts said, "and I could always throw strikes, even as a kid."

He was pitching college-league ball in Vermont in the summer of 1947 when the scouts began clearing their throats around him. Six clubs invited him to come and work out in September—the

Roberts at Michigan State in 1947

Phillies, Yankees, Red Sox, Tigers, Athletics, and Braves.

The Phillies saw him first. After watching him throw, the consensus was: Don't let this kid out of the park. They agreed on a $25,000 signing bonus and Robin Roberts was a Phillie.

They started him out with Wilmington (Delaware) in the Interstate League. After two months and a 9–1 record, he was brought up.

Though Roberts was just 7–9 on his maiden voyage through the big leagues, the judgments passed upon him were unanimous: Here was a coming star. Everyone, from fans to players to umpires to the press, agreed. Roberts impressed them all with his fast ball, his control, his effortless delivery, and his poise.

This young pitching jewel also had another facet, one that could not be taught or cultivated: He seemed to have a deep reservoir of strength, from which he summoned resources as he needed them.

"He was not a strikeout pitcher per se," Sawyer said. (Roberts never fanned as many as 200 in a season.) "He might get three or four a game, but they always seemed to come with a man on third and less than two out. And when he had a lead late in the game, you just couldn't get it away from him."

Right-hander Gene Conley, for several years a Phillies teammate of Roberts, recalled a conversation with Robin in which he had an insight into athletic resolution that impressed even Conley, who was not only a big-league pitcher but also a professional basketballer with the Boston Celtics:

I asked him one time "Robby, when you've got a runner on third and you need some extra on the ball, do you find yourself pushing off that mound a little harder?"

"No," he said. "I pitch the same all the time. The first pitch goes in the same way as the last one."

"That can't be true," [Conley] said, "because I notice when there's a man on third and less than two out, that ball pops a little better."

"Well," he said, "you can't see what I'm doing. That comes from within."

From within. The unpretentious Roberts probably didn't realize how much he was saying, how decisive was the line he was drawing not just between athletes and mere mortals, but also between athletes and mere athletes. There was an elite in the game that faced pressure not

Roberts was with Houston in 1965–66

with grace but with something much more primitive, with a sort of primal fury, as though being challenged this way was insulting.

Roberts not only felt this expansive power "within," he gave vivid demonstrations of its tangible impact, and never more tellingly than at Brooklyn's Ebbets Field on September 30, 1950. On their way to a fairly easy pennant, the Phillies had suddenly run into a September minefield that cost them pitcher after pitcher (to injury and military service) and, consequently, their once-comfortable lead. What it came down to on that September 30 was a one-game margin over the Dodgers with one game to play—against the Dodgers at Ebbets Field.

With most of his starting pitching not available, a desperate Eddie Sawyer had turned to his ace with greater and greater frequency. For what was the Philadelphia Phillies' biggest game in 35 years, Sawyer went once more to Robin Roberts, asking his overworked ace to pitch it and avert a three-game pennant playoff for which the Phillies would not have starting pitchers.

"There was nobody else," Sawyer said. "And anyway, I wouldn't have wanted anybody else."

"That was the biggest game I was ever involved in," Roberts said. "It was going to be my fourth start in eight days, and for some mysterious reason, whether it was youth or enthusiasm or whatever, I had as good stuff on that eighth day as I'd ever had. I should have been worn out, but I wasn't."

Going deeper and deeper "within," Roberts kept finding the stamina to go on, and he needed every ounce of it, for he was matched with Dodger ace Don Newcombe, at the top of his form that day. It was a sizzling 1–1 duel for nine innings, with a breathtaking bottom of the ninth that saw the Dodgers have the winning run thrown out at the plate and then the indefatigable Roberts have to extricate himself from a one-out, bases-loaded situation, which he did by retiring two splendid hitters, Carl Furillo and Gil Hodges.

In the top of the 10th inning, the Phillies' Dick Sisler shot a three-run homer into the left-field stands to throw a ribbon around it for the Phillies, the knot of which Roberts tied in the last of the 10th, giving the Phillies their first pennant since 1915.

That stunning performance, a landmark game in Philadelphia baseball history, gave Roberts his 20th victory of the

With Baltimore in 1963

A rare picture of Roberts in a New York Yankees uniform. He was with the Yankees for spring training in 1962 but was released before the season opened.

season (against 11 defeats) and marked the beginning of six consecutive seasons in that coveted circle for him. He was 21–15 the next year and then in 1952 reached his peak with a 28–7 record, following that with marks of 23–16, 23–15, and 23–14.

From 1952 through 1954, Roberts started 116 games and completed 92 of them, averaging over 330 innings and about one base on balls every six innings.

"It was a combination of his natural strength, sharp control, and easy delivery than enabled him to pitch so much, and so effectively," Sawyer said. "Of course, with his control and his reluctance to throw at hitters, he was tagged for quite a few home runs, but I don't remember too many of those coming in the late innings of close games."

After six years of heavy labor on the mound, Roberts, thirty years old in 1956, began a slow decline. After leading the league in wins for four straight years, he now walked the other side of the street for two years, leading in losses in 1956 (18) and 1957 (22), though he did have 19 wins in '56.

After three more seasons of reasonably good productivity, he dropped to a horrendous 1–10 record in 1961 and was sold to the Yankees after the season. The Yankees released him at the end of spring training, and he signed with Baltimore. In 1962 he was 10–9 for the Orioles, but his 2.78 ERA was the American League's second-lowest. He gave the Orioles two more good years (14–13, 13–7) before being released at the end of July 1965. He signed with the Houston Astros a week later and pitched for them until the following July. He finished his big-league career with the Chicago Cubs in 1966, ending with a lifetime record of 286–245.

In the mid-1970s, a writer came by to interview Eddie Sawyer. The former Phillies manager laughed when asked "that grand old question": If your life depended on your winning one game, who

Roberts with the Chicago Cubs at the end of 1966, his final big-league season

would you want to see on the mound for you?

"That's easy," Sawyer said. "Give me Robin Roberts."

Phillies manager Eddie Sawyer

Whitey illustrating the fact of his 25th victory in 1961

WHITEY FORD

To his teammate and closest friend, Mickey Mantle, Whitey Ford was "the greatest pitcher that ever lived." While the statement contains a generous lacing of friendship and loyalty, one must also take into account that the two were teammates for 15 years, during which Mantle watched Ford run up a 236–106 won-lost record, which works out to a .690 winning percentage, highest of any pitcher in the twentieth century.

The glitter of that winning percentage is an example of what happens when a great pitcher has every advantage going for him. Whitey spent the bulk of his career pitching for winning teams (he, of course, was one of the reasons they were winning teams), in a ball park whose dimensions were singularly ideal for him. Add to this Ford's artful carving on the mound, his assortment of sharp and swooping breaking pitches (some of which, he admitted later, were slightly "doctored"), his excellent control, his innate savvy, his gritty resolve under pres-

sure, and you have, well, modern baseball's hardest pitcher to defeat.

Mantle called him "Slick," and while it applied to Whitey's pitching, what Mickey was referring to was the smarts Whitey had absorbed from the sidewalks of New York, where he was born on October 21, 1928. To Mickey Mantle of Commerce, Oklahoma, Edward Charles Ford was the embodiment of the quick-thinking, quick-witted, coolly confident city slicker of talk and tale.

Closer to cocky than boastful, Ford took the mound with an abiding inner conviction that he was going to win, and the tougher the going, the more important the game, the better he got. Not a big man (he was 5'10"), not blessed with blazing speed, he mastered the art of putting his pitches where he wanted to, compelling the batters to hit them where he wanted them to, which was on the ground or, in Yankee Stadium's generous outfield, to the expanses of left and center.

Whitey was pitching on the sandlots of

To Mickey Mantle, Whitey was "the greatest pitcher that ever lived."

Queens when he perked the interest of the Yankees, Brooklyn Dodgers, and Boston Red Sox. The interest, however, was modest, and when the Yankees offered a bonus of $7,000, the other clubs moved aside.

The eighteen-year-old left-hander began his career with the Butler (Pennsylvania) club in the Mid-Atlantic League. His progress through the large, well-stocked Yankee farm system was steady rather than spectacular. A 13–4 season with Butler earned him a jump to Norfolk

in the Piedmont League, where he was 16–8. A year later he was with Binghamton (New York) in the Eastern League, showing a 16–5 record. In 1950 he was with Kansas City in the American Association, a phone call away from the big leagues. The call came after he had gone 6–3.

Joining the Yankees in the midst of a torrid pennant race with the Tigers and Red Sox, the always self-assured Ford broke in so impeccably that he set an American League record—most consecutive victories at the start of a career, with nine.

Teammate Eddie Lopat, himself a star left-hander, remembered the impression the new man made:

His true test came late in the season, against Detroit, the club we were battling neck-and-neck with at the time. We were caught short for a pitcher to open that series. So Stengel and Jim Turner, our pitching coach, said, "Well, we might as well see what the young fellow is made of," and they started him against Dizzy Trout. Whitey battled him 1–1 into the top of the ninth. Then we scored eight runs and Whitey won it easily. As far as we were concerned, that was his true test. He'd proved he could pitch under pressure.

Ford lost his final decision in 1950, giving him a 9–1 record, helping the Yankees into the World Series. He beat the Phillies in the fourth and final game of the Series, allowing no earned runs in 8⅔ innings.

After that high-speed debut, Ford entered military service for two years. He came back in 1953, raised an 18–6 record, and soon was the ace of the staff.

Pitching with what he once described as a pitcher's three essentials—"arm,

Whitey Ford in 1950, right off the sidewalks of New York

heart, and head"—Ford was 16–8, 18–7, and 19–6 the next three seasons, leading with a 2.47 ERA in 1956.

The reason the nearly unbeatable Ford was not the consistent 20–game winner he should have been was due to the special handling he received from Stengel. The Yankee manager had adopted the tactic of holding his ace out of the rotation in order to spot him against certain opponents, usually the opposition's top pitcher—which makes Ford's won-lost record even more impressive. "It seemed," one writer recalled, "like he was always pitching against Bob Lemon or Billy Pierce or Jim Bunning or some other top gun. And beating them. He beat everybody."

In 1961 Ralph Houk replaced Stengel as manager, and one of his moves was to insert and maintain Ford in the regular rotation. As a result Ford started more games than he ever had before (39, most in the league), pitched more innings (283, most in the league), and turned in his greatest season (25–4, including a 14-game winning streak). He was the Cy Young Award winner that year. After a "disappointing" 17–8 year in 1962, he came back with a 24–7 record in 1963.

Ford, who had tied a major-league record with two successive one-hitters in early September 1955, had his most memorable moments in the heat of World Series play. He appeared in 11 World Series and three times (1955, 1960, 1961) had 2–0 records. He worked in enough October shootouts to be the all-time leader in both games won (10) and games lost (8).

Ford's most prominent achievement was a run of scoreless innings he pitched in World Series competition in 1960, 1961, and 1962. In 1960 he logged 18 straight goose-egg innings when he blanked the Pirates twice. In 1961 he pitched another shutout against the Reds, then five more runless innings in a game he had to leave after suffering an injury. It was during this game that he broke Babe Ruth's record of $29\frac{1}{3}$ consecutive scoreless innings in World Series play, which Ruth had established in the World War I era. Ford went on to extend his string to $33\frac{2}{3}$ straight zeros in the opening game of the 1962 Series against the San Francisco Giants before being scored on in the second inning.

In 1966 a circulatory blockage in his left shoulder held him to a 2–5 record, disabling him from August 22 through the end of the season. Ford's problems were symbolic. He had been the Yankees' ace through the team's most successful era.

The starting pitchers for the first game of the 1964 World Series, Whitey Ford *(left)* and Ray Sadecki.

Mickey Mantle, Ford's closest friend on the Yankees

His physical problems coincided with the decline of a 45-year dynasty, with the departures of Mantle, Elston Howard, Roger Maris, Bobby Richardson, and other pillars of the Yankee success.

Ford came back after surgery in 1967, or tried to. He pitched well, his 2–4 record notwithstanding. But his shoulder continued to bother him, and he also was experiencing severe pain in his elbow when he pitched.

Pitching against the Tigers in Detroit one night at the end of May, he had to walk off the mound, unable to tolerate the pain any longer. When his teammates filed into the clubhouse after the game, he was gone, his locker empty. The greatest pitcher in New York Yankee history had retired.

Brooklyn Dodgers rookie Sandy Koufax in 1955

SANDY KOUFAX

When it comes to discussions of baseball's greatest players, there is seldom unanimity; the variables and the imponderables operate at too many levels. Nevertheless, when it came to choosing the premier pitcher of the 1960s, from a group that included Bob Gibson, Whitey Ford, Don Drysdale, Juan Marichal, and Ferguson Jenkins, only the most benighted would have disputed the selection of Sandy Koufax. There were even those who felt that Koufax was unequaled among pitchers of the postwar era, and some of their arguments were puncture proof. So formidable were Koufax's exploits that they were virtual culminations of modern pitching, leading some encomiasts to rank him ahead of Waddell, Grove, Hubbell, and Spahn as the greatest left-hander of all time. Once they start talking about you in those terms, you can't lose.

There are, however, a couple of negatives usually mentioned in discussions of Koufax's career. One is the fact that it took him so long to achieve stardom—he came up in 1955, and it wasn't until 1961 that he became a force in the league. True enough, but there was one important mitigating factor: When the nineteen-year-old recipient of a $20,000 bonus joined the Brooklyn Dodgers in 1955 there was a rule mandating that bonus players who had received in excess of $6,000 for signing had to remain with the big-league club for two years. This made Koufax a major leaguer before he was ready, and because the Dodgers were a contending club, the youngster seldom had an opportunity to pitch, which retarded his development for years. It was three years before he took the mound with any degree of regularity.

The second negative concerns the relative brevity of his career. Although he spent 12 years in the major leagues, only six of them can be considered of stellar quality. (His record for his first six years was 36–40. But in 692 innings he had 683 strikeouts, alerting the Dodgers to the

Sandy Koufax at the University of Cincinnati

many quality seasons as Dizzy Dean, whose demigod status has never been challenged, and that his years of success were so high voltage, dominating, and record setting that it simply doesn't matter how few or how many they were.

Koufax was born in Brooklyn on December 30, 1935. His original ambition was to be an architect, and when he attended the University of Cincinnati his favorite sport was basketball. But baseball, and specifically pitching, was his destiny, and the smoke signals set off by his fast ball attracted the scouts. He signed his bonus contract with the Dodgers on December 22, 1954, the Brooklyn club giving itself a Christmas present of undreamed of proportions, although it would be in Los Angeles that it would be finally unwrapped.

But first the young man had to grind himself into a pitcher. In the beginning he wasn't just wild, he was spectacularly wild. "Taking batting practice against him," one Dodger said at the time, "is like playing Russian roulette with five bullets." When manager Walter Alston first saw the new recruit in spring training in 1955, "He was in a little warmup area behind the barracks playing catch with somebody. They were about sixty feet apart, and I would say about half his return throws were going over the other guy's head. I looked at that and said to myself, 'What the hell have we got here?' "

What they had was a strong young left-hander with lethal speed and not the first inkling of what to do with it. When he got the ball over the plate he was seldom hit—his two victories in 1955 were both shutouts. Getting it over with enough frequency was the problem.

fact that there was more than a pulse beat in that left arm.) This negative is countered by the fact that Koufax had as

It took year after year of gritty, de-

The New York papers took note of Koufax's record-breaking performance against the Yankees in the 1963 World Series.

termined work. Koufax was relentless in his determination to succeed, and the Dodgers were reluctant to give up on him. "The tipoff was," Alston said, "whenever we talked trade with other clubs, his was the first name they mentioned."

Koufax finally realized that the "less-was-more" syndrome applied to his pitching. Instead of gripping the ball tighter and trying to throw it harder when he got in a jam, he learned to relax on the mound. "Trying to use super speed when he got into trouble was what was hurting him," coach Joe Becker said. "His muscles tightened up so he couldn't throw pro-

perly." When Sandy threw with a loose, relaxed wrist, Becker said, "his pitches did things."

One of the things they did was go over the plate. But Koufax was not content just to throw strikes; he was intent on pitching to spots, the essence of true control pitching.

Koufax began his ascent to greatness after the club moved to Los Angeles. In 1958 he was 11–11, a year later 8–6, then 8–13, averaging better than a strikeout per inning. On August 31, 1959, he struck out 18 in a game. With the 13 he had fanned in his previous start, he es-

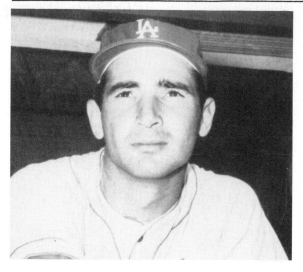

"They just stopped hitting him."

tablished a new two-game record of 31. The 18 strikeouts tied Bob Feller's major-league record.

In 1961 he began approaching stage center with an 18–13 record and 269 strikeouts, which exceeded by two the National League record set by Christy Mathewson in 1903.

In 1962 it all began centering perfectly for him. He was putting the ball where he wanted to, that sizzling fast ball and crackling overhand curve. "When you have that kind of stuff and that kind of control," Alston said, "well, they just stopped hitting him."

A circulation problem in his finger cost him a third of the 1962 season, but Koufax still rang up a 14–7 record, 216 strikeouts in 184 innings, and a 2.54 earned run average, the first of his record-making five successive ERA titles. On April 24 he again fanned 18 in a game, victimizing the Chicago Cubs, and on June 30 he no-hit the New York Mets.

A year later he reached the moutaintop. He posted a 25–5 season, leading in wins, with an ERA of 1.88, 306 strikeouts,

and 11 shutouts, the latter a major-league record for left-handers. On May 11, he no-hit the San Francisco Giants. He capped the year with two wins over the Yankees in the Dodgers' four-game sweep of the World Series, including a blazing 15 strikeouts in the opener, setting a new Series record (since broken). His glittering year earned him both the Cy Young and Most Valuable Player awards.

The following year he was 19–5, a hand injury costing him about a dozen starts. He led with a 1.74 ERA and seven shutouts. The by-now annual no-hitter came on June 4, against the Phillies.

Already being troubled by a degenerative arthritic condition in his left elbow that would soon abort his career, he sealed the legend of his greatness with pure fire in 1965 and 1966.

In 1965 he was 26–8, took his fourth straight ERA title with a 2.04 figure, led with 27 complete games, 336 innings pitched, and a new single-season strikeout record of 382 (later broken by Nolan Ryan). A fourth no-hitter came on September 9, against the Cubs, and this time it was a perfect game, a 1–0 victory over Bob Hendley, who hurled a one-hitter in defeat. In his flawless effort, Koufax fanned 14, including the final six. It was only the second perfect game in modern National League history, the Phillies' Jim Bunning having pitched one the year before against the Mets. The game also established a new major-league mark for no-hitters, and although Nolan Ryan later pitched five of these gems, Koufax remains the only man to have four no-hitters in the same league.

In the World Series against the Minnesota Twins, he was 2–1, with both victories shutouts, including a seventh-

Koufax pitching to the Minnesota Twins' Tony Oliva in the 1965 World Series

Dodger manager Walter Alston *(left)* and Koufax

game world-championship performance. He was again the Cy Young Award winner.

With most great players the talk is of statistics; with Koufax it is records, and they continued to fall upon him like stardust. He was the acknowledged titan of big-league pitchers; he was special; he stood apart from the others as no pitcher had since Feller. He was described by one big-league manager as being "like a professional playing with amateurs."

Koufax was a highly polished young man. He went to concerts and the theater, ate in the best restaurants (ballplayers are not generally known for gourmet tastes), golfed at exclusive clubs, read good books. Among the frantic splendors and glaring lights of Hollywood he maintained his privacy and was known as a loner. He could have owned the boulevards of the movie capital, been a celebrity prince, but he wanted none of it.

"He knew who he was," one writer said. "When he was out on the mound Sandy gave everything he had, but when the game was over he seemed to melt away with them, get back to himself, or maybe his other self."

Milwaukee pitcher Gene Conley told of the time the Braves were filing into Dodger Stadium for a night game and encountered in the runway their opponent of the evening, Sandy Koufax.

"He stopped and shook hands and said hello to all of us," Conley said. "Just as nice and polite as could be. When we got into the dressing room, somebody said, 'Isn't he a nice guy?' Then somebody else said, 'If he's such a nice guy, then why is he going to strike out fifteen of us tonight?' "

Indeed, there seemed to be two of him—the one mild and friendly; the other, the man on the mound, as intense and furiously resolved a pitcher as ever lived, drawing from a deep well of stamina that dazzled batters in the eighth and ninth innings of close games.

"He threw harder in the ninth inning of a close game than he did in the first," Alston said. "It was an amazing thing to see, a man getting stronger and stronger, as strong as he had to be. Who else was that way? You can name them on one hand: Bob Feller, Robin Roberts, Bob Gibson, and they said Lefty Grove could pitch like that."

In 1966 he was 27–9, setting a games-won record for National League left-handers (later tied by Steve Carlton), leading with 317 strikeouts, five shutouts, 27 complete games, and 1.73 ERA; he won his third Cy Young Award. (It should be noted that Koufax won his three Cy Youngs in the days when there was only one such award handed out in big-league baseball; it wasn't until 1967 that it was decided to designate a winner in each league. And it is possible to go even further in gilding the image of this left-handed pitcher: Not only was he selected three times as the premier pitcher in all baseball, but each time the vote was unanimous.)

He was 0–1 in the 1966 World Series as the Dodgers were swept by the Baltimore Orioles. In four World Series (he started a game in the 1959 Series against the White Sox) he was 4–3, with an 0.95 ERA for 57 innings, across which he gave just 36 hits and struck out 61.

For the five years beginning in 1962 he was 111–34, as near to unbeatable as a big-league pitcher has been. He had five straight ERA titles (a record); four no-hitters, including a perfect game; numerous strikeout records; winning seasons of 25, 26, and 27; and he was by far baseball's number-one drawing card. He was thirty years old.

But it was over. The arthritic condition in his left elbow had continued to degenerate. He often suffered excruciating pain after a game. He had to take painkillers, apply burning salves to the elbow, bathe it in ice water for as long as 40 minutes. And it kept getting worse. He was warned that continued pitching could ultimately cost him use of the arm. And so that winter he retired, and all the rest that might have been—how many more wins, how many more strikeouts, shutouts, no-hitters, perfect games, ERA titles, Cy Young Awards—was left to the realm of speculation, along with the empty seasons of Dizzy Dean and the lost years of Bob Feller. He left, as one dreamy writer put it, "at high noon, a Hamlet in mid-soliloquy."

The searing fast balls and the back-breaking curves added up to 165 wins, 87 losses, and, in 2,324 innings, 2,396 strikeouts.

In 1985, almost fifty years old, Koufax took the mound in spring training to throw some batting practice for the Dodgers. He was clocked at over 90 miles an hour.

The greatest pitcher of the postwar era

Bob Gibson: An "implacable" competitor

BOB GIBSON

ob Gibson was born in Omaha, Nebraska, on November 9, 1935, son of a mill worker who died before the boy was born, leaving behind a widow to raise seven children in the city's black ghetto. ("I didn't know it was a ghetto until I came out of it," Gibson said later.) He was a sickly child, fighting off bouts of pneumonia, asthma, rickets, and a rheumatic heart, among other things. He emerged from this shaky childhood to grow into a tough 6'1", 195-pound athlete of strength, speed, grace, and coordination, all of which was enhanced by the incandescent determination that signals the highest achievers.

Gibson was a performing personality on the mound, though not in the extroverted sense of a Dizzy Dean; he was more in the mold of a Sandy Koufax in the intensity of his concentration, in the riveting competitive aura he projected. Sitting in the stands, one could fairly sense the cauldron of emotions in the glowering, tightly focused Gibson, in his quick, almost peevishly impatient windup, in the searing zeal of his deliveries, and in the hurtling thrust of his follow-through.

He was known to throw in tight to batters, claiming possession of the inside corner, and if necessary targeting a batter. When was it necessary? "The only times I've hit a man," he said, "is after one of our guys has been hit." Hit deliberately, he meant. Ballplayers generally know when the hitting of a batsman has not been accidental, and any pitcher who low-bridged a Cardinal batter when Gibson was working was asking for sizzling retaliation. One National Leaguer said, "I always winced when one of our pitchers plugged a Cardinal when Gibby was pitching, because I knew one of us was going to answer for it."

Growing up in the ghetto, growing up black in a predominantly white society, left an indelible impression. Much of the fire Gibson displayed on the mound was no doubt the surface of smoldering resentments stoked early and continually.

Rookie right-hander Bob Gibson in 1959

No one ever truly leaves the ghetto, not in the psychic sense. The fame and success Gibson came to know as an ace pitcher was like trying to cover sandpaper with silken threads; the underlying, hard-grained angers could never be assuaged.

Bob Gibson on the mound, glaring down at the batter with withering contempt, was one stunningly complex man. He was the pure athlete, he was the implacable competitor, and he was the black man with those ever-unresolved conflicts born of the Omaha ghetto. He was also, in his own blunt way, significantly part of baseball's civil-rights movement, taking the rudimentary beginnings of Jackie Robinson's revolution to more diversified levels of progress. Bob Gibson was one of the first black pitchers to unabashedly deck white (as well as black) hitters without concern for

creating an "incident," without concern for anyone accusing him of anything other than aggressively operating within baseball's guidelines. This was a most rugged form of progress, but progress it was.

He had little patience with bores or fools, whether they were fans, reporters, or fellow ballplayers. To deal with Gibson, one writer said, "You had better know your facts, have some understanding of his personality, and be to the point. He could be the perfect interview—intelligent and articulate—until or unless you went down the wrong lane with him, like going on assumptions or hearsay."

He was an all-around athlete at Omaha Technical High, playing baseball and basketball as well as appearing with the track team. From there he went to Omaha's Creighton University, where he was a standout on the basketball team. (He was adept enough at the sport to tour one winter with the Harlem Globetrotters.) He was also on Creighton's baseball team, primarily as an outfielder but

Bob Gibson

Gibson *(right)* with Henry Aaron

beginning to make the transition to the mound, for the very sound reason that "I felt I could get to the majors fastest as a pitcher."

Gibson did not graduate from Creighton; instead, in 1957, he accepted a $4,000 bonus from the Cardinals and was assigned to his hometown team in Omaha. This was Triple-A ball, the American Association, quite a fast start for a rookie. The twenty-one-year-old fast baller just about held his own, posting a 2–1 record and 4.29 earned run average for 42 innings. He was then sent down to the Columbus (Georgia) club in the South Atlantic League and had a 4–3 record. He was also exposed to some backwater, slack-jawed prejudice, hearing that blacks were referred to as "alligator bait" and facing the indignities of "colored-only" rest rooms and drinking fountains. They were piled onto the other, earlier learning experiences that a black youth—ghetto or otherwise—undergoes, and so there was little to round the sharp edges of Gibson's resentment or cool the heat that fueled him.

In 1958, splitting the season between Omaha and Rochester, the latter in the swift currents of the International League, Gibson was a combined 8–9. There was thus far nothing in his statistics to suggest that this young man was going to become the Cardinals' greatest pitcher since Dizzy Dean. Nevertheless, the front office liked the young man's fast ball and brought him up to the majors in 1959.

Gibson started the '59 season with Omaha, going 9–9 when he was called up in July. In his first big-league start, on July 30, 1959, he shut out the Cincinnati Reds, 1–0. The rest of the season, however, was less glittering, and he wound up 3–5.

Gibson started the 1960 season with Rochester, but the Cardinals soon brought him back, this time to stay. Splitting his time between the bullpen and the starting rotation, he was 3–6.

Gibson traces his ascent to stardom to the arrival of Johnny Keane as Cardinal manager in July 1961 (Bob was less than enamored of previous skipper Solly Hemus). Keane, who had been Gibson's first manager in professional ball at Omaha in 1957, put him in the rotation to stay, and the fast baller responded by finishing with a 13–12 record. Thereafter for the next five years, his win totals increased with each passing season, from 13 to 15, 18, 19, 20, and 21.

In 1964 his 19–12 record helped the Cardinals to their first pennant since 1946, won by a single game over the second-place Reds and Phillies. Gibson was bedrock coming down the stretch, winning nine of his final 11 decisions, including the pennant winner on the last day of the season.

Bob Gibson is arguably the greatest pitcher in World Series history, with nine starts in three Series (1964, 1967, 1968), eight complete games, a 7–2 record, and 81 innings of work in which he allowed

The Cardinals' greatest pitcher since Dizzy Dean

just 55 hits, had 92 strikeouts, and posted an ERA of 1.89.

In his first World Series, against the Yankees in 1964, he was 2–1, losing the second game but winning both game five (in 10 innings) and, on two days rest, the seventh and final game.

By 1966 Gibson was a full-fledged star. In 1962 he had begun striking out over 200 batters a season, reaching a peak of 270 in 1965, at the time a league record for right-handed pitchers.

He was in the midst of another strong season in 1967 when on July 13 a line drive off the bat of Pittsburgh's Roberto Clemente hit him and broke his leg. (The gritty Gibson tried to remain in the game, even pitched to another batter, before being taken out.) It was assumed he would be lost for the season, but he was back in six weeks, ending with a 13–7 record and

helping the Cardinals to another pennant.

Gibson was never more awesome than in the 1967 World Series against the Boston Red Sox. He won the opener 2–1, striking out 10. In game four he shut the Sox out, 6–0. Working the seventh game, he three-hit the Sox in a 7–2 win, again fanning 10 and, just for good luck, hitting a home run. Overall, he held the Red Sox to just 14 hits in 27 innings.

In 1968 Gibson pitched the Cardinals to another pennant, turning in a landmark season, a season for future aspirants to greatness to measure themselves against. His won-lost record (22–9) was standard for an ace (at one point early in the season he stood at 3–5), but his ERA was not standard for anybody; it was, in fact, record-making. With a 1.12 ERA, Gibson established a major-league record for the lowest earned run average for a pitcher with 300 or more innings (he pitched 305).

Gibson's 1968 season is a glittering tiara of accomplishments. Along with the paucity of runs surrendered, he led the league with 268 strikeouts and 13 shutouts, and only Grover Cleveland Alexander, with 16 blankers in 1916, ever had more in a big-league season. In the month of June, Gibson hurled five shutouts, had a string of 48 straight scoreless innings and then 95 innings during which he gave up just two runs. At one point he had 15 consecutive wins. He completed 28 of 34 starts and was never once driven from the mound in the middle of an inning.

Gibson continued his rush in the World Series that year against Detroit. In the opener he fired a 4–0 shutout (defeating 31-game winner Dennis McLain in a heralded matchup) and set a new Series

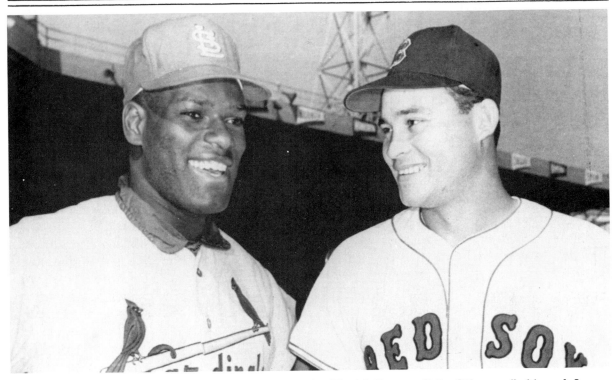

Starting pitchers for the first game of the 1967 World Series, Bob Gibson *(left)* and Jose Santiago

record with 17 strikeouts. To illustrate how high the fires were burning within him that day, Gibson went into the bottom of the ninth needing two whiffs to break Sandy Koufax's Series record of 15—and got them, plus one more.

In game four, Gibson again beat the Tigers, 10–1, fanning 10, for a record seventh-straight World Series victory. He lost game seven, however, by a score of 4–1. Locked in an 0–0 tie with Mickey Lolich in the top of the seventh inning, Gibson gave up three runs, largely due to a misplayed fly ball by center fielder Curt Flood.

His scintillating 1968 season earned Gibson both Most Valuable Player and Cy Young Award honors.

In 1969 the Cardinal ace came back with a 20–13 season and in 1970 posted his best won-lost record with a 23–7 mark, earning his second Cy Young Award. It was his fifth and final 20-game season, although he was 19–11 in 1972, his last big winning year. He fanned over 200 batters again that year, for the ninth time, setting a new major-league record (later broken by Nolan Ryan and Tom Seaver).

With the heat cooling on his fast ball and slider, and the jagged edge of his curve beginning to dull, Gibson waned to 12–10 and 11–13 records in 1973 and 1974 and ended his career with an uncharacteristic 3–10 in 1975.

His career totals are 251–174, including a no-hitter against Pittsburgh on August 14, 1971, and 3,117 strikeouts, which at the end of the 1986 season had him ninth on the all-time list.

Juan Marichal: "It looked like he had one long, continuous leg, with a spiked shoe on either end."

JUAN MARICHAL

If the vagaries of baseball lore have established one thing it is that a man can win 243 big-league games (against just 142 losses), win over 20 games in a season six times, strike out over 200 batters in a season six times, lead the league in shutouts twice, lead in earned run average, pitch a no-hitter—and end up being remembered most vividly for hitting another player over the head with a bat.

Thus, the most graphic memory in the Hall of Fame career of Juan Marichal, San Francisco Giants ace of the 1960s who was the near equal of Sandy Koufax, was the day he raised knobs on the head of the Dodgers' Johnny Roseboro.

The date was August 22, 1965, the place Candlestick Park in San Francisco. The Dodgers and Giants were engaged in a simmering pennant race (which the Dodgers were to win by two games), it was a hot day, there had been some controversial plays and rancorous verbal exchanges the previous two days, and the two clubs had never enjoyed a tranquil

relationship anyway. On this slightly overcooked August Sunday Marichal had raised temperatures a bit higher by delivering pitches that had come close to making Dodgers Maury Wills and Ron Fairly each a head shorter.

"When I came to the plate, I expected to go down," Marichal said. "I knew how they were feeling. They were mad at me. I expected Koufax to throw at me."

The great Koufax was indeed on the mound for the Dodgers, but he was averse to throwing at batters, knowing that with his high-velocity fast ball he could inflict serious damage. So he chose not to indulge in this quaint baseball custom. (Koufax was not alone in this aversion to committing potential manslaughter; it was shared by other members of the pitching elite, most notably Bob Feller, Tom Seaver, and Robin Roberts.) Nevertheless, Marichal was expecting to be targeted, and indeed he was, except that the ball came from another direction.

In returning one of Koufax's pitches,

Dodger catcher John Roseboro fired it so close to Marichal's head that Juan later claimed the ball actually nicked his ear.

"I turned back and said, 'Why did you do that?' He didn't give any reason. He made two moves, two steps, to me. When I saw him come after me with a chest protector and a mask, I hit him with the bat." Solidly, too; enough to cut Roseboro's head and cover his face with blood, bringing both teams rushing onto the field.

It was one of baseball's more brutal scenes, and it left a permanent stain on the record of one of its most elegant pitchers. Marichal was subsequently fined $1,750 by league president Warren Giles and suspended for eight days. Roseboro later sued Marichal for $110,000 and reportedly agreed to a $7,500 out-of-court settlement in 1970. (The two combatants later became good friends.)

Marichal's behavior that day was out of character in the extreme. No one would have argued with this description of Juan, offered by a close friend: "Basically, a nice, average guy . . . about as nice a human being as you will meet."

Marichal was born on October 20, 1938, in the town of Laguna Verde, in the northwest corner of the Dominican Republic, near the blue Caribbean waters where he became expert at spearfishing and catching lobsters.

Growing up, young Juan received his first baseball instruction from an older brother who had played some semipro ball. Later, he spent two years in the Dominican air force, pitching for its baseball team. When he left the air force, Marichal was a highly polished pitcher.

In 1957, the Giants' Caribbean scout Alex Pompez brought the young man to the club's attention. Pompez's report read, in part, "He is devout, he reads the Bible constantly. He has a beautiful delivery. Nobody taught him anything." The Giants respected the youngster's devotion to scripture, but they were more impressed with the esthetics of his delivery. In October 1957, they signed him for a $500 bonus.

When farm director Carl Hubbell saw the new recruit in the spring of 1958, he immediately gave instructions to everyone: Do not tamper with the boy's delivery. There was a grace and purity and power to Marichal's style that was immediately eye-catching.

"He looked and acted like a veteran out

Juan Marichal, "the Dominican Dandy"

The notorious Marichal-Roseboro incident. Marichal has just struck Roseboro and is raising the bat menacingly. Sandy Koufax is in the center, having just run down from the mound.

there, from day one," one scout recalled.

What they were seeing was the high-kick delivery that was soon to become familiar on the mounds of the National League. Marichal would rear far back on his right foot and kick the left skyward, sometimes tipping back so far and raising his left leg so high that for a moment it looked as though he had one long, continuous leg, with a spiked shoe on either end, tilting so extremely that his right hand often was inches above the ground.

He threw overhand, three-quarters, and sidearm, and he threw fast balls, curves, sliders, screwballs, and changes, with masterful control of all. According to Frank Robinson, you could face Marichal four times in the same game and "never see the same pitch thrown from the same delivery to the same spot."

When Henry Aaron was asked which was Marichal's best pitch, he replied, "He doesn't have any one best pitch. Let's just say when he has to—or wants to—strike you out, he's got the pitch."

Marichal broke in with a 21–8 record for Michigan City in the Midwest League. This was in 1958. A year later he was

The Yankees' Whitey Ford *(left)* and Marichal, who started the fourth game of the 1962 World Series

18–13 with Springfield (Massachusetts) in the Eastern League. In 1960 he began the year with the Giants' top farm club, Tacoma in the Pacific Coast League. Sporting an 11–5 record in mid-July, he was promoted to the big team.

Marichal served fair notice in his first big-league start, against the Phillies on July 19, 1960. The twenty-one-year-old rookie hurled 7⅔ innings of no-hit ball, gave up a single to Clay Dalrymple, and finished with the first one-hit debut in major-league history. It was a high-speed start to one of the finest pitching careers ever.

Marichal finished 1960 with a 6–2 record. He was 13–10 in 1961 and a year later was 18–11 as he helped pitch the Giants into the World Series. It was to be his only Series appearance, and his lone start was aborted by an injury. Starting the fourth game against the Yankees, he had thrown four shutout innings when he suffered an injury to his finger while attempting to bunt in the top of the fifth.

Marichal bloomed to full stardom in 1963 with a 25–8 record, 2.41 ERA and 248 strikeouts. The next three years he had won-lost figures of 21–8, 22–13, and 25–6 (leading with 10 shutouts in 1965). After an injury-hampered 1967, when he was 14–10, he came back with records of 26–9 in 1968 and 21–11 in 1969. He was the first National League right-hander since Grover Cleveland Alexander a half century before to win 25 or more games three times. Nevertheless, Marichal remains, in the words of one writer, "the greatest pitcher never to win a Cy Young Award."

It was Marichal's misfortune to be pitching contemporaneously with Koufax, the acknowledged titan of all postwar pitchers. Whatever Marichal did, Koufax did better (five straight ERA titles from 1962 through 1966). Between 1963 and 1966, Marichal had a 93–35 won-lost record, Koufax 97–27; Marichal averaged 229 strikeouts and six shutouts during these seasons, Koufax 307 and eight.

Koufax retired after the 1966 season, but when Marichal had his superb 26–9 record in 1968, he ran into Bob Gibson's buzz-saw 1.12 ERA year and again lost

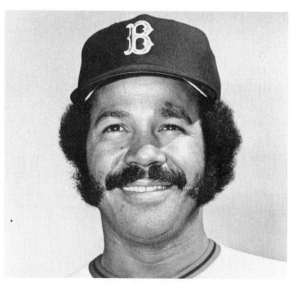

Marichal with the Red Sox in 1974

Marichal about to fire

the Cy Young Award. In 1969, when he was 21–11 with a league-leading 2.10 ERA, Juan lost out to Tom Seaver's 25–7 season.

Nevertheless, "the Dominican Dandy" (as, inevitably, he came to be called) had his long career of enduring splendor, sequined with special moments. Among them were his no-hitter against the Houston Colts (as they were then known) on June 15, 1963, and two weeks after that a 1–0, 16-inning win over Warren Spahn during which Marichal delivered 227 pitches. At one point in his career, in late May 1967, he owned a career record of 138–61, which figured out to a .693 winning percentage, highest in baseball his-

tory. (His final winning percentage is a sterling .631.)

Marichal's last big winning season was 1971, when he was 18–11. After slipping to 6–16 and 11–15 the next two years, he was sold to the Boston Red Sox in December 1973. Held to a 5–1 record because of injuries, he was released by the Sox in the spring of 1975. Ironically, his final big-league season saw him getting into two games with the Dodgers, with whom he had engaged in his infamous brawl 10 years earlier. After losing his final big-league decision, Marichal was released and returned to the Dominican Republic, where he remains revered as one of that nation's greatest sports heroes.

Palmer in 1977

JIM PALMER

Tall, handsome, intelligent, articulate, personable. A rare combination of blessings, and Jim Palmer possessed them all. But rarer yet was the gift that looks could not cajole nor wit call forth: a blazing fast ball with a hop on it.

This abundantly gifted man and athlete was also the beneficiary of a privileged childhood. The adopted son of wealthy New York parents (Palmer was born in New York City on October 15, 1945), he divided his formative years between a Park Avenue apartment and the bucolic tranquility of Upstate retreats. Part of the Palmer legend is that his earliest experiences at doing what few men were ever able to do as well—throwing a baseball—came upon manicured lawns in Upstate New York, with the family butler serving as his catcher.

Upon the death of his father, Jim's mother remarried and the family moved to Beverly Hills, and then to Scottsdale, Arizona. Here the future Hall of Famer went to high school, lettering in baseball, football, and basketball. That high, rising fast ball, searing the dry southwestern air, caught the attention of big-league scouts, and a year after graduating from high school Jim signed a $65,000 bonus contract with the Baltimore Orioles.

The eighteen-year-old youngster reported to the Aberdeen (South Dakota) club in the Northern League. An 11–3 record elevated him to the Orioles a year later. He broke into 27 games with Baltimore in 1965, mostly as a reliever, posting a 5–4 record.

In 1966, at the age of twenty, Palmer moved into Baltimore's starting rotation, turning in a 15–10 record and helping the club to the pennant. In the second game of the World Series he allowed just four hits in shutting out the Dodgers 6–0, becoming the youngest man ever to pitch a shutout in the October pageant.

So young Jim Palmer was riding one of the most enviable crests available—baseball stardom. It wasn't just his 15–10 record; it was what baseball men saw when he went into his graceful, loose-jointed windup and popped that fast ball. They saw a superbly equipped young pitcher who was going to get better and better. He was one of the game's prized assets.

But then came one of those sudden demonstrations of just how fragile and vulnerable a pitcher's arm can be. Soon after pitching a one-hitter against the Yankees in May 1967, Palmer hurt his arm and found himself in an abrupt and frightening plunge from the stars to the grass roots.

"My arm was practically useless for a year," he said, "and it scared the hell out of me." He was, in fact, written off by many baseball men as another of the game's sadly aborted careers.

The injury gouged two years from his

Baltimore rookie right-hander Jim Palmer in 1965

career. The Orioles sent him to the minors, at one point as far down as Miami in the Florida State League, where they hoped the hot weather would help bake out his problems. Excruciating pain in his arm and shoulder limited him to 37 minor-league innings in 1968, divided between Miami, Rochester in the International League, and Elmira in the Eastern League. He was left unprotected in the baseball draft, but no club thought him worth the gamble.

By the spring of 1969, however, the pain was gone and the stylish young right-hander was firing the ball with his former authority. He made a dazzling comeback with a 16–4 record, throwing six shutouts along the way. Six weeks on the disabled list (the injury was unrelated to his previous problems) kept him from his first 20-game season. His victories included a no-hitter against Oakland on August 13.

A year later, in 1970, Palmer pitched himself high into the galaxy of stars, with a 20–10 season, working a league-leading 305 innings and delivering five shutouts, also a league high. He capped off his season by defeating Minnesota in the third game of Baltimore's sweep of the league-championship series and then scoring another postseason victory against Cincinnati in the World Series.

The following three years saw Palmer pitching as steadily as a summer rain, with records of 20–9, 21–10, and 22–9, culminating in a Cy Young Award in the latter year, 1973, in which he led the American League with a 2.40 earned run average.

Injuries slowed him to a 7–12 record in 1974, but he then returned with another run of four straight 20–game seasons. In 1975, arguably his greatest year, he was 23–11, leading in victories, ERA (2.09), and shutouts (10). It brought him his second Cy Young Award.

In 1976, he won his third Cy Young Award, on the strength of a 22–13 record, his win total the best in the league. He followed this with a 20–11 record in 1977 (again leading in wins) and 21–12 in 1978, his eighth and final 20-game season. He is the only American League right-hander to amass so many 20-game seasons in the lively-ball era.

After 1978, Palmer's win totals began leveling. In 1979 he was 10–6, then 16–10, 7–8, 15–5, 5–4, and finally 0–3 in 1984, his final season. He ended his career with a 268–152 record and 2.86 lifetime ERA, a remarkably low figure for the lively-ball era.

Despite the sizzle on his fast one, Palmer was not known as a strikeout pitcher, never fanning as many as 200 in a year. It was his preference to let the batters hit the ball; it was easier on the arm. And in his heyday seasons with the Orioles he had behind him some of the finest defense in baseball history, most notably Brooks Robinson at third, Mark Belanger at shortstop, and Paul Blair in center field.

With Palmer as the acknowledged ace of a staff that included 20-game winners Dave McNally and Mike Cuellar—in 1971 Pat Dobson joined with them to give the Orioles four 20-game winners, only the second time this has happened (the other club was the 1920 Chicago White Sox)—the Orioles were perennial contenders and frequent winners. In six league-championship series Palmer was 4–1, in six World Series, 4–2.

Palmer was a frank and outspoken man, with a clear perspective on things. When asked if he considered himself an intellectual, he said, "Never. I read and

Jim Palmer

Palmer *(left)* loosening up at Baltimore's Miami spring-training camp in 1974

think like most functioning human be-ings. If I had to describe myself, it would be as an objectivist. I like fact, logic, real-ity. Abstract ideas go over my head, and deceitful institutions like politics bore me. I enjoy books about the mind."

Palmer's relationship with his longtime (15 years) manager Earl Weaver was one of baseball's more amusing, adversarial, and fascinating associations. They were as antithetical as it is possible for two men to be. Weaver was short, feisty, emo-tional, explosive, rough edged—a career minor leaguer who made it to the top as a manager and became one of the most successful ever. Palmer was tall, in-telligent, well-spoken, by baseball stan-dards a patrician. Both were strong willed and opinionated. Both were con-vinced they knew what was best for pitcher Jim Palmer, and these convictions did not always coincide.

Weaver seemed always in awe of his ace. Sometimes the skipper sounded like a parent at once proud of and ex-asperated by a brilliant but recalcitrant son.

"If he'd listen to me," Earl said on more than one occasion, "he'd win thirty games a year. He's capable of it. But he thinks he's too perfect to listen to me."

Palmer saw this attitude as victimiz-ing, that the "perfectionist syndrome" worked to his disadvantage. "I have to pitch with more pressure than I should because other people are unrealistic,

Jim Palmer

Earl Weaver

irrational," he said. "They look at irrelevant things—I've won a lot, I'm outspoken, I'm the big name on the club, I'm nice looking—and they construe it to mean I shouldn't lose. The best I can hope for is consistency. I'm a realist about myself, and one thing I *can't* be is perfect."

Palmer's feelings about Weaver were a blend of respect (for Earl's baseball acumen), annoyance (with Earl's sometimes overly emotional outbursts), and impatience (with Earl's advice, opinions, and criticism). Nevertheless, "I like Earl," Palmer said, "I really do. I understand him. Both of us like to win, we're emotional, we're stubborn, and we speak our minds."

Speak their minds they did, and never more incisively than to one another. There was the occasion in Arlington, Texas, when Earl came charging out to the mound to berate Palmer for throwing "the wrong pitch" (which had been hit for a double). Fed up with Earl's badgering, Jim handed his glove to the skipper and said, "Here, *you* pitch if you can do better."

After the inning, Palmer said, Weaver

Palmer with his first two Cy Young Awards

"started jumping up and down like a maniac, cursing and berating me for showing *him* up."

Jim Palmer and Earl Weaver each made their separate but distinct ways into baseball lore, and each left behind the definitive word about the other.

"Earl's a great manager," said Palmer.

"Jim's a Hall of Famer," said Weaver.

Steve Carlton

STEVE CARLTON

"I n this game," one baseball man said, "when you refer to 'Lefty,' and everybody knows who you're talking about, it's pretty damned impressive." This was in the early 1980s, and the Lefty he was talking about was Philadelphia's Steve Carlton.

The impression Carlton made on baseball's consciousness in the 1970s and 1980s was doubly profound, for not only was he one of the game's few truly dominant pitchers (the only one to win four Cy Young Awards), but he was also a personality that was perceived by certain segments of the press and public as decidedly odd, if not downright eccentric. In an age when media exposure was relentless, with print and electronic journalists demanding ever more access to a player and his thoughts, Carlton cut off all communication between himself and the journalists.

This silence was not the sullenness shown by some surly and insecure athletes, nor was it the hostility of certain natural-born clods striking a pose. As far as Carlton was concerned, his taciturnity had a very rational grounding. The big left-hander had been engaging in some new mental and physical disciplines that he believed would help his concentration on the mound and consequently his performance. According to the story that circulated after Carlton shut the zipper on future interviews, some writers had quoted him out of context on his theories, depicting him, in Carlton's opinion, as woolly-headed and pretentious. Rather than risk further vulnerability to the jibes and snickers of the press, Carlton simply clammed up. And he was most resolute in this posture: After the Phillies had won the 1980 World Series and their clubhouse was the scene of the usual media swarm, Carlton chose to remain off bounds in the trainer's room rather than risk dropping a syllable within range of possible journalistic hearing.

No doubt the sum of the world's wisdom is diminished not a jot because Steve Carlton refused to confide in the sporting press. Nevertheless, he was known to be a highly intelligent man, articulate, well-read, and insightful.

That a man in late-twentieth-century America could tell the press to take a hike and still remain at the top of his profession must have made every politico in and out of office gnaw with envy. None of those politicos, of course, could throw the slider the way Carlton did: The pitch was there when you began your swing but had gone somewhere else when you finished.

Carlton was born in Miami, Florida, on December 22, 1944. He grew tall, 6'4", and rangy, filling out to an enormously strong 210 pounds. Part of the Carlton "eccentricity" was the excruciating physical regimen he subjected himself to; among these exercises was pushing and twisting his arms in a deep tub of rice. He was also a highly skilled exponent of the martial arts. How much all of this contributed to the hurry on his fast ball and the bite of his slider is left to conjecture. But this is plain fact: Among National League left-handers, he stands with Hubbell, Spahn, and Koufax.

He signed with the St. Louis Cardinals for a $5,000 bonus and began his professional career with Rock Hill (South Carolina) in the Western Carolinas League in 1964. After a 10–1 start, promotion was swift, to Winnipeg and Tulsa later that season, then 15 games with the Cardinals in 1965, a split season with Tulsa and St. Louis in 1966, and, starting

"In this game, when you refer to 'Lefty,' and everybody knows who you're talking about, it's pretty damned impressive."

in 1967, a regular spot in the Cardinal rotation.

Carlton had seasons of 14–9 in 1967, 13–11 in 1968 (helping the Cardinals to pennants in each of those years), and 17–11 in 1969.

Carlton's most celebrated single game came on September 15, 1969, against the New York Mets, then on their celestial highway to a "miracle" pennant. On this night Carlton struck out 19 Mets but lost the game 4–3 to a pair of two-run home runs by Ron Swoboda. The game left Carlton with a clutch of records: most strikeouts in a single game, major leagues (later broken by Roger Clemens); most strikeouts in a game, National League (later tied by Tom Seaver); most strikeouts in a game by a left-hander, major leagues; most strikeouts in a night game, National League; most strikeouts in a game by a losing pitcher, National League. One big night of glory and irony.

After the 1969 season Carlton got into a salary dispute with his employers. He finally signed a reported $90,000 two-year contract, but the haggling left Cardinals owner August Busch feeling somewhat moody about his forthright young southpaw.

Carlton delivered seasons of 10–19 and then 20–9 as his part of the deal. When he began negotiations for his next contract, the Cardinals focused on the 10–19 while Steve's eye saw the 20–9. The negotiations were not going well when suddenly on February 25, 1972, in what was perhaps a moment of pique, or exasperation, or maybe an insight beyond the ken of the rest of the world, the Cardinals traded Carlton to the Phillies for Rick Wise, an estimable right-hander but far short of the world-class status Carlton was immediately to achieve.

The 1972 season was to be for Carlton what 1941 and .406 were for Ted Williams, or 1961 and 61 home runs were for Roger Maris. It was a summer of spectacular pitching, the monument that will always bulk large over a long and noteworthy career.

First, the self-speaking statistics: 27 wins, 10 losses; 346 innings pitched; 310 strikeouts; 1.98 earned run average; 30 complete games; 8 shutouts; a 15-game winning streak; 22 victories in his last 25 starts. His 27 wins tied the league record for a left-hander set by Koufax in 1966.

This was an extraordinary season under any circumstances, but Carlton's circumstances were these: He was pitching for a last-place team that ended with a 59–97 record (no other Phillies pitcher

Carlton with the Chicago White Sox, with whom he finished the 1986 season

Carlton pitching for the San Francisco Giants in 1986

fourth Cy Young Award with a 23–11 record. He slipped to 15–16 in 1983 but led the league in strikeouts for the fifth time.

In 1984 he was 13–7, and at the age of thirty-nine pitched his fewest innings, 229 (not counting the strike season) since 1967. It was a telltale statistic, for Carlton, seemingly indestructible and immune to the incursions of time, had begun suffering from back and arm problems. These problems conspired to reduce the great left-hander to a 1–8 record in 1985, his miseries driving him to the disabled list for the first time in his career, a restriction that lasted eight weeks.

In June 1986 the Phillies released Carlton, after he had compiled a 4–8 record and wretched 6.18 ERA. He then began a wandering not unfamiliar to veteran

won more than seven games), meaning he came close to winning 50 percent of his team's games. It all added up to his first Cy Young Award.

After three relatively disappointing seasons, Carlton came back to a sharp 20–7 record in 1976 and then took another Cy Young plaque in 1977 with a 23–10 mark. He hit another peak in 1980, going 24–9 and winning his third Cy Young Award.

The 1981 players' strike, which shut down the major leagues for about a third of the season, probably cost Carlton another 20-game year, as he finished at 13–4. In 1982 he picked up his unprecedented

Steve Carlton, signed by the Cleveland Indians in the spring of 1987

ballplayers whose pride and resolve keep them from the shades of retirement. He signed with the San Francisco Giants in early July, pitched a month (to a 1–3 record), was released and then signed by the Chicago White Sox, with whom he was 4–3. The White Sox did not re-sign him, and he went to spring training with the Phillies in 1987 but did not make the staff. The Cleveland Indians signed him just as the season was opening, later sending him to the pennant-contending Minnesota Twins in a midseason transaction.

Going into the 1987 season, Carlton had compiled a 323–229 lifetime record, with 4,040 strikeouts, second only to Nolan Ryan on the all-time scrolls. He had been a 20-game winner six times, a strikeout leader five times. In five league-championship series he was 4–2, and in four World Series 2–2.

Throughout much of his career of more than two decades, Carlton maintained his singularity, ignoring the press, abiding by his own inner rhythms, becoming the game's most determined and notable sphinx. But to baseball fans it was irrelevant whether he was reticent or verbose; all that mattered was what he accomplished on the mound, throwing his fast ball and that slider, which some hitters said was baseball's least-hittable pitch. His accomplishments, as consistent as they were lustrous, built Steve Carlton into one of the game's pitching marvels, the man who was "Lefty" on the playing fields of baseball America.

Carlton with the Phillies in 1972, the year he was 27–10

The Mets Rookie-of-the-Year-to-be, Tom Seaver, in the spring of 1967

TOM SEAVER

He has been called the greatest right-handed pitcher to work in New York since Mathewson. That is a broad claim, covering the greater part of the century, four teams (Dodgers, Giants, Yankees, and Mets), and a number of eminent pitchers. Nevertheless, it is a highly defensible assertion.

Seaver was "a full package." In addition to his mighty pitching, he was boyishly handsome, intelligent, shrewdly analytical about his craft, witty, telegenic, married to an equally telegenic blonde of sparkling beauty. He was the main generator in the raising of a team of bumbling, downtrodden reputation to a world championship, a team that came on suddenly and unexpectedly like a force of nature, the team known as "the Miracle Mets of 1969." If there was something magical about him, well, that perception was not totally incorrect, since the Mets had quite literally pulled him from a hat.

Seaver was born on November 17, 1944, in Fresno, California. After a stint in the Marine Corps, which he joined when he was eighteen years old, he enrolled in the University of Southern California, where he began pitching for the baseball team. The scouts soon began coming around, moths attracted by the fire of Seaver's low, rising fast ball, which shot out of a classically compact windup and powerfully coordinated delivery with terrific emphasis on leg thrust. (Throughout his career, Seaver was always a profound student and exponent of pitching mechanics.)

For two years he discouraged the scouts, intent on pursuing his education. When the Atlanta Braves laid siege with a $40,000 bonus offer, however, he succumbed. This was in February 1966. But it was soon brought to the attention of baseball commissioner William Eckert that the signing was in technical violation of a college rule, and the contract was nullified, with Seaver being declared a free agent.

Tom Seaver

Eckert ruled that any club (other than the Braves) that was willing to match the terms of the voided contract was now eligible to sign the young fast baller. Only three teams expressed interest—Cleveland, Philadelphia, and the New York Mets. Accordingly, on April 3, 1966, the names of these three teams were written on slips of paper and dropped into a hat, and one was drawn by Eckert. It was the Mets, who promptly signed Seaver for a reported $50,000 bonus and assigned him to their Jacksonville, Florida, club in the International League. The architecture of the coming "Miracle of 1969" was as chancy as that.

So the twenty-one-year-old Californian was starting pro ball in the fast lane of Triple-A. He compiled a creditable 12–12 record, with 188 strikeouts in 210 innings, and, an eye-catching statistic for a young pitcher, just 66 bases on balls. It earned

him a trip to the Mets' spring-training camp in 1967, where he made the team.

Pitching for a club still enduring the throes of seemingly hopeless, albeit charming, ineptitude, a club that lost 101 games and finished last, Seaver put together a solid 16–13 record and 2.76 earned run average. It brought him the league's Rookie of the Year designation.

In 1968, pitching for a club that finished ninth, but with an improved 73–89 won-lost record, Seaver was 16–12, with a sharp 2.20 ERA, five shutouts, just 48 bases on balls in 278 innings, and 205 strikeouts. Those strikeouts marked the beginning of what was to become a long and impressively achieved pair of records—the major-league standards for most years with 200 or more strikeouts (10) and most consecutive seasons with 200 or more strikeouts (9), 1968 through 1976.

And then came 1969, that vintage year for made-in-America miracles. First Neil Armstrong set foot on the moon; then the New York Mets made an even less probable journey (baseball style), rising from ninth place to the championship of the world. The main booster rocket in the Mets' ascension was Tom Seaver, with a 25–7 record, 2.21 ERA, a World Series vic-

Seaver (left) with Dodgers ace Don Drysdale

Seaver *(right)* with Mets teammate Joe Torre and friend

tory over the Baltimore Orioles, and a Cy Young Award.

Seaver's career continued in strong tidal flow, with year after year of high-winning, high-strikeout, low ERA seasons. He was a 20-game winner in 1971, 1972, 1975, and 1977; he led in ERA in 1970, 1971, and 1973; he led in strikeouts in 1970, 1971, 1973, 1975, and 1976. He won two more Cy Young Awards, in 1973 and 1975.

On April 22, 1970, he put on one of the most thrilling and dominating pitching performances in major-league history, tying the major-league record for strikeouts in a single game by fanning 19 San Diego Padres, and setting one of the most enthralling pitching records of all time by striking out the final 10 batters in succession.

With his fast ball and hard slider, Seaver was a power pitcher, but one with finesse. "Pitching, to me," he said, "is throwing strikes, and throwing strikes down low. To be able to throw a fast ball on the inside part of the plate and then be able to throw a fast ball on the outside part of the plate, within a realm of two or three inches—that's big-league control."

He went to the mound with a sense of purpose that was almost esthetic in its design. "As a pitcher, I feel I'm creating something," he said. "Pitching itself is not enjoyable while you're doing it. Pitching is work. I don't enjoy it until I can stand back and look at what I've created."

He also found the challenge stimulating: "That classic duel between pitcher and batter is fascinating. No other sport has such a vivid and dramatic confrontation. I live my life around the four days between starts."

In the spring of 1977, Seaver and the Mets began a dispute over his contract (he wanted to renegotiate, they did not)

Seaver *(left)* with the recently retired Sandy Koufax

that grew more and more acrimonious. Finally, on June 15, he asked to be traded, and the club obliged him, dealing him to Cincinnati.

The Mets have long been derided for making "one of the worst trades in baseball history" when they dealt a young Nolan Ryan to the California Angels in 1971. Indeed it was an unfortunate transaction; but in other ways the Seaver deal was just as bad. He was by now in his 11th year with the Mets, an acknowledged superstar, already acclaimed as one of the all-time pitching greats. He was "Tom Terrific" and "the Franchise," with the latter nickname carrying weight both real and symbolic in 1977. The Mets were back in the second division again, a struggling club, and about all the fans had to cling to was Seaver, baseball's reigning king of the hill. Possessing him had been a significant point of pride. Failing to come to terms with their ace and then peevishly trading him cost the club heavily in credibility with its fans.

Seaver prospered in Cincinnati, posting a combined 21–6 record for the Mets and Reds, leading the league with seven shutouts. It was the last of his five 20-game seasons. On June 16, 1978, he pitched his only no-hitter, against the Cardinals. A year later his 16–6 record helped the Reds to a division title, though they lost in the league-championship series to Pittsburgh.

In the strike-shortened 1981 season, Seaver had a 14–2 record, leading the league in victories (for the third time).

After injuries had riddled his 1982 season, dropping him to a 5–13 record, Seaver was dealt back to the Mets. Pitching for a last-place club, the now thirty-eight-year-old right-hander was 9–14.

In January 1984, operating under the theory that no one would be interested in an aging pitcher with a high salary and diminishing prospects, the Mets left Seaver exposed to the compensation pool draft, then in effect as part of the strike-settling agreement of 1981. The Mets were wrong. The Seaver magic still glowed brightly, particularly in the minds of the Chicago White Sox, who selected him, to the dismay of both Seaver and the Mets.

With the Cincinnati Reds in 1980

Yogi Berra watches Tom Seaver warm up in the Shea bullpen in 1973.

After 17 years, Seaver now changed leagues. In 1984 he gave the White Sox a fine 15–11 year. In 1985 he was 16–11. Among his victories that season was his landmark 300th, on August 4. Appropriately, it was recorded in New York, against the Yankees at Yankee Stadium.

The following June he was traded to the Boston Red Sox, whom he helped pitch to a division title. A knee injury kept him out of the league-championship series and also the World Series, depriving baseball of what would have been a dramatic confrontation with the National League–champion Mets. It also spared New York City a nagging case of schizophrenia, for as one long-time Mets fan put it, "I couldn't have rooted against him. But on the other hand . . ."

After failing to come to contractual agreement with the Red Sox for the 1987 season, Seaver found himself out of baseball for the first time in 21 years. Early in the season, however, finding themselves with an injury-depleted pitching staff, the Mets asked him to come back. After working out for several weeks, Seaver realized "it was no longer there," and retired from baseball, leaving behind a 311–205 lifetime record.

For two decades Tom Seaver had brought brilliance, style, and distinction to baseball, on the diamond and off. He had brought the New York Mets credibility and led them to victory. Not since Babe Ruth created the Yankees image and carried them to success in the 1920s had any single player done so much for, and meant so much to, a big-league franchise.

Tom Seaver

"THEY ALSO RAN"

The more exclusive one makes a list of the "best" or the "greatest," the higher the standards. Nevertheless, there are a number of other pitchers whose careers mandate acknowledgment in these pages. They are, in fact, legitimate members of the pitching hierarchy, and if the primary list had been expanded many of the following would have been mustered.

Joe (Iron Man) McGinnity earned his nickname by pitching doubleheaders and generally working tirelessly throughout his 10-year career (1899–1908). The right-hander was a two-time 30-game winner for John McGraw's Giants at the turn of the century and had a lifetime record of 247–144.

Addie Joss was Cleveland's ace right-hander from 1902–1910, when he died suddenly of complications caused by tubercular meningitis, at the age of thirty-one. In an era of low earned run averages, Addie's were among the lowest; in fact, his lifetime ERA of 1.88 is second in baseball history to Ed Walsh's

1.82. Joss, who completed 234 of his 260 starts, was a 20-game winner four times and had a lifetime compilation of 160–97.

Right-hander Burleigh Grimes was Dazzy Vance's co-ace on the Brooklyn Dodgers in the 1920s. Grimes, who was known as a spitballer but who claimed his best pitch was his fast ball, worked in the big leagues from 1916 through 1934. He was a 20-game winner five times and overall was 270–212.

Old-time ballplayers remembered southpaw Herb Pennock as one of the smoothest pitchers of his time, and for Herb it was a long time indeed: He pitched in the American League from 1912 to 1934, having his greatest years with the juggernaut Yankee teams of the 1920s. Twice a 20-game winner, Pennock's lifetime slate reads 240–162.

"If Ted Lyons had pitched for the Yankees," Joe McCarthy said, "he would have won 400 games." But Ted didn't pitch for the Yankees. He was employed by the Chicago White Sox, from 1923 to 1946, during which time he won 260 and lost 230, including three 20-game seasons.

Ferguson Jenkins was one of the great pitchers of his age, but it was an age in which he often found himself overshadowed by Juan Marichal, Bob Gibson, and Tom Seaver. The big right-hander was a seven-time 20-game winner, including six straight seasons for the Chicago Cubs (1967–1972). His lifetime record is 284–226.

Right-hander Gaylord Perry pitched for eight different teams from 1962 to 1983 and emerged from it all as one of those rarest of overachievers—a 300-game winner. Overall, he stands at 314–265. At his retirement in 1983, he was third on the all-time strikeout list, with 3,534, and fourth in innings pitched, with 5,351. A five-time 20-game winner, Perry is the only man to win a Cy Young Award in each league—with Cleveland in 1972 and San Diego in 1978.

One of the most remarkable of all major-league pitchers, Nolan Ryan was still throwing his fast ball over 90 miles an hour at the age for forty in the 1987 season, his 21st in the big leagues. For Ryan, it was a season of truly impressive achievements. Despite an 8–16 record, he led the National League in strikeouts (270) and earned run average (2.76). The all-time strikeout leader, with 4,547 (after the 1987 season), Ryan holds numerous records, including the single-season record of 383 whiffs (1973), five years with 300 or more strikeouts, and his astonishing five no-hitters. On the dark side of Ryan's ledger, the thing that has kept him from scaling pitching's ultimate heights, is his wildness. His 2,355 bases on balls (after the 1987 season) are by far the most in baseball history; eight times he led the league in free tickets, twice issuing over 200 in a season. This liberality has held the otherwise nearly unhittable Ryan to a lifetime 261–242 record (after the 1987 season).

LIFETIME RECORDS

Statistics reprinted by permission of the *Sporting News.*

Cy Young

Year	Club	League	G	IP	W	L	Pct	H	R	SO	BB	CG	ShO
1890—Canton		Tri-State	31	260	15	15	.500	253	165	201	33	......	0
1890—Cleveland		National	17	150	9	7	.563	145	83	36	32	16	0
1891—Cleveland		National	54	430	27	20	.574	436	239	146	132	44	0
1892—Cleveland		National	53	455	36	11	.766	362	159	167	114	48	9
1893—Cleveland		National	53	426	32	16	.667	441	229	102	104	42	1
1894—Cleveland		National	52	409	25	22	.532	493	266	101	101	44	2
1895—Cleveland		National	47	373	35	10	.778	371	176	120	77	36	4
1896—Cleveland		National	51	414	29	16	.644	467	212	137	64	42	5
1897—Cleveland		National	47	338	21	18	.538	389	195	87	50	36	2
1898—Cleveland		National	46	378	25	14	.641	394	174	107	40	40	1
1899—St. Louis		National	44	369	26	15	.634	364	170	112	43	40	4
1900—St. Louis		National	41	321	20	18	.526	337	146	119	38	32	4
1901—Boston		American	43	371	33	10	.767	320	113	159	38	38	5
1902—Boston		American	45	386	32	10	.762	337	137	166	51	41	3
1903—Boston		American	40	342	28	10	.737	292	116	183	37	34	7
1904—Boston		American	43	380	26	16	.619	326	104	203	28	40	10
1905—Boston		American	38	321	18	19	.486	245	98	208	30	31	5
1906—Boston		American	39	288	13	21	382	289	135	146	27	28	0
1907—Boston		American	43	343	22	15	.595	287	101	148	52	33	6
1908—Boston		American	36	299	21	11	.656	230	68	150	37	30	3
1909—Cleveland		American	35	295	19	15	.559	267	110	109	59	30	3
1910—Cleveland		American	21	163	7	10	.412	149	62	58	27	14	1
1911—Cleveland		American	7	46	3	4	.429	54	28	20	13	4	0
1911—Boston		National	11	80	4	5	.444	83	47	35	15	8	2
American League Totals			390	3234	222	141	.612	2796	1072	1550	399	323	43
National League Totals			516	4143	289	172	.627	4282	2096	1269	810	428	34
Major League Totals			906	7377	511	313	.620	7078	3168	2819	1209	751	77

Rube Waddell

Year	Club	League	G	IP	W	L	Pct	H	R	SO	BB	CG	ShO
1897—Louisville		National	2	13	0	1	.000	13	7	5	6	1	0
1898—Detroit		Western	9			4	4	.500	61		31	30	......	......
1899—Col.-Grand Rapids		American	42	330	27	13	.675	......	154	......	......	......	......
1899—Louisville		National	10	80	7	2	.778	71	38	41	16	9	1
1900—Pittsburgh		National	29	212	9	11	.450	186	101	133	53	16	2
1900—Milwaukee		American	15	129	10	3	.769	90	28	75	20	13	2
1901—Pittsburgh–Chicago		National	31	250	13	16	.448	252	136	167	67	26	0
1902—Los Angeles		Pacific Coast	20	178	12	8	.600	128	66	142	37	19	2
1902—Philadelphia		American	33	275	23	7	.767	224	89	210	67	26	3
1903—Philadelphia		American	39	323	21	16	.568	271	112	301	74	34	4
1904—Philadelphia		American	46	384	25	19	.568	309	111	349	81	39	8
1905—Philadelphia		American	46	324	26	11	.703	230	86	286	91	27	7
1906—Philadelphia		American	43	272	15	17	.469	219	89	203	88	22	8
1907—Philadelphia		American	44	285	19	13	.594	247	120	226	72	20	7
1908—St. Louis		American	43	286	19	14	.576	223	93	232	90	25	5
1909—St. Louis		American	31	220	11	14	.440	204	78	141	57	16	5
1910—St. Louis		American	10	34	3	1	.750	31	19	16	9	0	0
1910—Newark		Eastern	15	97	5	3	.625	73	......	53	41	......	......
1911—Minneapolis		Amer. Assn.	54	300	20	17	.541	262	133	185	96	......	......
1912—Minneapolis		Amer. Assn.	33	151	12	6	.667	138	67	113	59	......	......
1913—Virginia		Northern	15	84	3	9	.250	86	......	82	20	......	......
American League Totals			335	2403	162	112	.591	1958	797	1964	329	209	47
National League Totals			72	555	29	30	.492	522	282	346	142	52	3
Major League Totals			407	2958	191	142	.574	2480	1079	2310	771	261	50

155

Christy Mathewson

Year Club	League	G	IP	W	L	Pct	ShO	H	R	ER	SO	BB	ERA
1899—Taunton	N. England	17	......	5	2	.714	......			......			......
1900—Norfolk	Virginia	22	187	20	2	.909	4	119	59	......	128	27	......
1900—New York	National	6	34	0	3	.000	0	34	32	......	15	20	......
1901—New York	National	40	336	20	17	.541	5	281	131	......	215	92	......
1902—New York	National	34	276	14	17	.452	8	241	114	......	162	74	......
1903—New York	National	45	367	30	13	.698	3	321	136	......	267	100	......
1904—New York	National	48	368	33	12	.733	4	306	120	......	212	78	......
1905—New York	National	43	339	31	9	.775	9	252	85	......	206	64	......
1906—New York	National	38	267	22	12	.647	7	262	100	......	128	77	......
1907—New York	National	41	315	24	12	.667	9	250	88	......	178	53	......
1908—New York	National	56	391	37	11	.771	12	281	85	......	259	42	......
1909—New York	National	37	274	25	6	.806	8	192	57	......	149	36	......
1910—New York	National	38	319	27	9	.750	2	291	98	......	190	57	......
1911—New York	National	45	307	26	13	.667	5	303	102	......	141	38	......
1912—New York	National	43	310	23	12	.657	0	311	107	73	134	34	2.12
1913—New York	National	40	306	25	11	.694	5	291	93	70	93	21	2.06
1914—New York	National	41	312	24	13	.648	5	314	133	104	80	23	3.00
1915—New York	National	27	186	8	14	.364	1	199	97	74	57	20	3.58
1916—N.Y.–Cinn.	National	13	74	4	4	.500	1	74	35	25	19	8	3.04
Major League Totals		635	4781	373	188	.665	83	4203	1613	......	2505	837	......

Eddie Plank

Year Club	League	G	IP	W	L	Pct	ShO	H	R	ER	SO	BB	ERA
1901—Philadelphia	American	33	262	17	11	.607	1	234	121	......	89	47	......
1902—Philadelphia	American	36	295	20	15	.571	1	300	139	......	110	64	......
1903—Philadelphia	American	43	338	23	16	.590	3	314	139	......	175	67	......
1904—Philadelphia	American	44	365	26	17	.605	7	307	112	......	209	77	......
1905—Philadelphia	American	41	346	25	12	.676	4	283	111	......	199	69	......
1906—Philadelphia	American	26	211	19	6	.760	5	160	53	......	102	51	......
1907—Philadelphia	American	43	344	24	16	.600	8	287	114	......	198	82	......
1908—Philadelphia	American	34	245	14	16	.467	4	202	71	......	135	46	......
1909—Philadelphia	American	34	265	19	10	.655	3	215	74	......	132	62	......
1910—Philadelphia	American	38	250	16	10	.615	2	218	89	......	123	55	......
1911—Philadelphia	American	40	257	22	8	.733	6	237	85	......	155	77	......
1912—Philadelphia	American	37	260	26	6	.813	5	234	90	......	110	83	......
1913—Philadelphia	American	41	244	18	10	.643	8	211	87	70	151	57	2.59
1914—Philadelphia	American	34	185	15	7	.682	4	178	68	59	110	42	2.87
1915—St. Louis	Federal	42	269	21	11	.656	6	210	75	60	145	58	2.01
1916—St. Louis	American	37	236	16	15	.516	3	203	78	61	88	67	2.33
1917—St. Louis	American	20	131	5	6	.455	1	105	39	26	26	38	1.79
Major League Totals		581	4234	305	181	.628	64	3688	1470	......	2112	984	......

"Three Finger" Brown

Year Club	League	G	IP	W	L	Pct	H	R	ER	SO	BB	ERA
1901—Terre Haute	I.I.I.	31	......	23	8	.742	198	......	......	138	41	......
1902—Omaha	Western	43	352	27	15	.643	309	......	......	140	82	......
1903—St. Louis	National	26	201	9	13	.409	231	105	......	83	59	......
1904—Chicago	National	26	212	15	10	.600	155	74	......	81	50	......
1905—Chicago	National	30	249	18	12	.600	219	89	......	89	44	......
1906—Chicago	National	36	278	26	6	.813	198	56	......	143	61	......
1907—Chicago	National	34	233	20	6	.769	180	51	......	107	40	......
1908—Chicago	National	44	312	29	9	.763	214	64	......	123	49	......
1909—Chicago	National	50	343	27	9	.750	246	78	......	172	53	......
1910—Chicago	National	46	295	25	14	.641	256	95	......	143	64	......
1911—Chicago	National	53	270	21	11	.656	267	110	......	129	55	......
1912—Chicago	National	15	89	5	6	.455	92	35	26	34	20	2.63
1913—Cincinnati	National	39	167	11	12	.478	174	79	56	41	44	3.02
1914—St. L.–Brooklyn	Federal	35	233	14	11	.560	233	106	80	118	61	3.09
1915—Chicago	Federal	35	238	17	8	.680	190	75	56	97	65	2.12

			G	IP	W	L	Pct	H	R		SO	BB		ERA
1916—Chicago	National		12	48	2	3	.400	52	27	21	21	9		3.94
1917—Columbus	Amer. Assoc.		30	185	10	12	.455	167	70	57	61	51		2.77
1918—Columbus	Amer. Assoc.		12	50	3	2	.600	49	18	15	13	9		2.70
1919—Terre Haute	I.I.I.		33	175	16	6	.727	161	69	56	72	20		2.88
1919—Indianapolis	Amer. Assoc.		6	34	0	3	.000	39	......		9	11		......
1920—Terre Haute	I.I.I.		13	80	4	6	.400	74	31	23	42	13		2.59
Federal League Totals			70	471	31	19	.620	423	181	136	215	126		2.60
National League Totals			411	2697	208	111	.652	2284	863	......	1166	548		......
Major League Totals			411	2697	208	111	.652	2284	863	......	1166	548		......

Ed Walsh

Year Club	League	G	IP	W	L	Pct	H	R	SO	BB	CG	ShO
1902—Wilkes-Barre	Pa. State	4	36	1	2	.333	31	......	20	8	......	......
1902—Meriden	Connecticut	21	182	15	5	.750	125	......	98	48	......	......
1903—Meriden	Connecticut	23	182	11	10	.524	135	......	126	46	......	......
1903—Newark	Eastern	19	117	9	5	.643	70	......	77	28	......	......
1904—Chicago	American	18	113	6	3	.667	83	37	52	34	6	1
1905—Chicago	American	22	138	8	3	.727	128	56	71	35	9	1
1906—Chicago	American	42	281	17	13	.567	214	90	171	58	24	10
1907—Chicago	American	56	419	24	18	.600	330	123	207	85	37	5
1908—Chicago	American	66	465	40	15	.727	343	111	269	56	42	12
1909—Chicago	American	31	230	15	11	.577	166	52	127	50	20	8
1910—Chicago	American	45	370	18	20	.474	242	90	258	61	33	7
1911—Chicago	American	56	369	27	18	.600	327	125	255	72	33	5
1912—Chicago	American	62	393	27	17	.614	332	125	254	94	32	6
1913—Chicago	American	16	98	8	3	.727	91	37	34	39	7	1
1914—Chicago	American	9	45	2	3	.400	33	19	14	20	3	1
1915—Chicago	American	3	27	3	0	1.000	18	4	12	6	3	1
1916—Chicago	American	2	3	0	1	.000	6	3	3	1	0	0
1917—Boston	National	4	18	0	1	.000	22	9	4	9	1	0
1919—Milwaukee	Amer. Assn.	4	21	2	2	.500	22	......	6	8		
1920—Bridgeport	Eastern	3	22	1	1	.500	22	......	6	6	......	......
American League Totals		428	2951	195	125	.609	2313	872	1727	611	249	58
National League Totals		4	18	0	1	.000	22	9	4	9	1	0
Major League Totals		432	2969	195	126	.607	2335	881	1731	620	250	58

Walter Johnson

Year Club	League	G	IP	W	L	Pct	ShO	H	R	ER	SO	BB	ERA
1907—Washington	American	14	110	5	9	.357	2	100	35	......	70	16	......
1908—Washington	American	36	257	14	14	.500	6	196	75	......	160	52	......
1909—Washington	American	40	297	13	25	.342	4	247	112	......	164	84	......
1910—Washington	American	45	374	25	17	.595	8	262	92	......	313	76	......
1911—Washington	American	40	322	25	13	.658	6	292	119	......	207	70	......
1912—Washington	American	50	368	32	12	.727	7	259	89	......	303	76	......
1913—Washington	American	48	346	36	7	.837	11	232	56	44	243	38	1.14
1914—Washington	American	51	372	28	18	.609	9	287	88	71	225	74	1.72
1915—Washington	American	47	337	27	13	.675	7	258	83	58	203	56	1.55
1916—Washington	American	48	371	25	20	.556	3	290	105	78	228	82	1.89
1917—Washington	American	47	328	23	16	.590	8	259	105	83	188	67	2.28
1918—Washington	American	39	325	23	13	.639	8	241	71	46	162	70	1.27
1919—Washington	American	39	290	20	14	.588	7	235	73	48	147	51	1.49
1920—Washington	American	21	144	8	10	.444	4	135	68	50	78	27	3.13
1921—Washington	American	35	264	17	14	.548	1	265	122	103	143	92	3.51
1922—Washington	American	41	280	15	16	.484	1	283	115	93	105	99	2.99
1923—Washington	American	42	261	17	12	.586	3	263	112	101	130	69	3.48
1924—Washington	American	38	278	23	7	.767	6	233	97	84	158	77	2.72
1925—Washington	American	30	229	20	7	.741	3	211	95	78	108	78	3.07
1926—Washington	American	33	262	15	16	.484	2	259	120	105	125	73	3.61
1927—Washington	American	18	108	5	6	.455	1	113	70	61	48	26	5.08
1928—Newark	International	1	0	0	0	.000	0	0	0	0	0	1	0.00
Major League Totals		802	5923	416	279	.599	110	4920	1902	1103	3508	1353	......

Grover Cleveland Alexander

Year	Club	League	G	IP	W	L	Pct	H	R	ER	SO	BB	ERA
1909—Galesburg	Ill.-Mo.		24	219	15	8	.652	124	49	......	198	42	....
1910—Syracuse	N. Y. State		43	245	29	14	.674	215	......	......	204	67	....
1911—Philadephia	National		48	366	28	13	.683	285	133	......	227	129	....
1912—Philadephia	National		46	310	19	17	.528	289	133	97	195	105	2.81
1913—Philadephia	National		47	306	22	8	.733	288	106	96	159	75	2.82
1914—Philadephia	National		46	355	27	15	.643	327	133	94	214	76	2.38
1915—Philadephia	National		49	376	31	10	.756	253	86	51	241	64	1.22
1916—Philadephia	National		48	390	33	12	.733	323	90	67	167	50	1.55
1917—Philadephia	National		45	387	30	13	.698	336	107	79	200	56	1.83
1918—Chicago	National		3	26	2	1	.667	19	7	5	15	3	1.73
1919—Chicago	National		30	235	16	11	.593	180	51	45	121	38	1.72
1920—Chicago	National		46	363	27	14	.659	335	96	77	173	69	1.91
1921—Chicago	National		31	252	15	13	.536	286	110	95	77	33	3.39
1922—Chicago	National		33	246	16	13	.552	283	111	99	48	34	3.62
1923—Chicago	National		39	305	22	12	.647	308	128	108	72	30	3.19
1924—Chicago	National		21	169	12	5	.706	183	82	57	33	25	3.03
1925—Chicago	National		32	236	15	11	.577	270	106	89	63	29	3.39
1926—Chicago–St. Louis	National		30	200	12	10	.545	191	83	68	47	31	3.06
1927—St. Louis	National		37	268	21	10	.677	261	94	75	48	38	2.52
1928—St. Louis	National		34	244	16	9	.640	262	106	91	59	37	3.36
1929—St. Louis	National		22	132	9	8	.529	149	65	57	33	23	3.89
1930—Philadelphia	National		9	22	0	3	.000	40	24	22	6	6	9.00
1930—Dallas	Texas		5	24	1	2	.333	35	23	22	4	11	8.25
Major League Totals			696	5188	373	208	.642	4868	1851	1372	2198	951	2.56

Dazzy Vance

Year	Club	League	G	IP	W	L	Pct	H	R	ER	SO	BB	ERA
1912—Red Cloud	Neb. State		36	......	11	15	.423	......	......	......	......	......	......
1913—Superior	Neb. State		25	......	11	14	.440	......	......	......	......	......	......
1914—Hastings	Neb. State		26	......	17	4	.810	......	......	......	194	71	......
1914—St. Joseph	Western		21	134	9	8	.529	129	64	44	108	50	2.96
1915—Pittsburgh	National		1	3	0	1	.000	3	3	3	0	5	6.00
1915—St. Joseph	Western		39	264	17	15	.531	224	118	86	199	110	2.93
1915—New York	American		8	28	0	3	.000	23	14	11	18	16	3.54
1916—Columbus	Amer. Assn.		14	50	2	2	.500	52	......	25	10	16	4.50
1917—Toledo	Amer. Assn.		15	71	2	6	.250	63	31	18	30	25	2.28
1917—Memphis	Southern		16	122	6	8	.429	102	41	......	61	28	......
1918—Memphis	Southern		16	117	8	6	.571	93	......	......	40	33	......
1918—Rochester	International		9	72	3	5	.375	85	39	31	34	23	3.88
1918—New York	American		2	2	0	0	.000	9	5	4	0	2	18.00
1919—Sacramento	Pacific Coast		48	294	10	18	.357	264	125	92	86	81	2.82
1920—Memphis–New Orleans	Southern		45	284	16	17	.485	253	104	......	65	65	......
1921—New Orleans	Southern		38	253	21	11	.656	225	115	99	163	80	3.52
1922—Brooklyn	National		36	246	18	12	.600	259	122	101	134	94	3.70
1923—Brooklyn	National		37	280	18	15	.545	263	127	109	197	100	3.50
1924—Brooklyn	National		35	309	28	6	.824	238	89	74	262	77	2.16
1925—Brooklyn	National		31	265	22	9	.710	247	115	104	221	66	3.53
1926—Brooklyn	National		24	169	9	10	.474	172	80	73	140	58	3.89
1927—Brooklyn	National		34	273	16	15	.516	242	98	82	184	69	2.70
1928—Brooklyn	National		38	280	22	10	.688	226	79	65	200	72	2.09
1929—Brooklyn	National		31	231	14	13	.519	244	110	100	126	47	3.90
1930—Brooklyn	National		35	259	17	15	.531	241	97	75	173	55	2.61
1931—Brooklyn	National		30	219	11	13	.458	221	99	82	150	53	3.37
1932—Brooklyn	National		27	176	12	11	.522	171	90	82	103	57	4.19
1933—St. Louis	National		28	99	6	2	.750	105	42	39	67	28	3.55
1934—Cincinnati–St. Louis	National		25	77	1	3	.250	90	47	39	42	25	4.56
1935—Brooklyn	National		20	51	3	2	.600	55	29	25	28	16	4.41
American League Totals			10	30	0	3	.000	32	19	15	18	18	4.50
National League Totals			432	2937	197	137	.590	2777	1227	1053	2027	822	3.23
Major League Totals			442	2967	197	140	.585	2809	1246	1068	2045	840	3.24

Lefty Grove

Year—Club	League	G	IP	W	L	Pct	H	R	ER	SO	BB	ERA
1920—Martinsburg	Blue Ridge	6	59	3	3	.500	30	16	......	60	24	
1920—Baltimore	International	19	123	12	2	.857	120	69	52	88	71	3.80
1921—Baltimore	International	47	313	25	10	.714	237	131	89	254	179	2.56
1922—Baltimore	International	41	209	18	8	.692	146	90	65	205	152	2.80
1923—Baltimore	International	52	303	27	10	.730	223	128	105	330	186	3.12
1924—Baltimore	International	47	236	27	6	.813	196	95	79	231	108	3.01
1925—Philadelphia	American	45	197	10	12	.455	207	120	104	116	131	4.75
1926—Philadelphia	American	45	258	13	13	.500	227	97	72	194	101	2.51
1927—Philadelphia	American	51	262	20	13	.606	251	116	93	174	79	3.19
1928—Philadelphia	American	39	262	24	8	.750	228	93	75	183	64	2.58
1929—Philadelphia	American	42	275	20	6	.769	278	104	86	170	81	2.81
1930—Philadelphia	American	50	291	28	5	.848	273	101	82	209	60	2.54
1931—Philadelphia	American	41	289	31	4	.886	249	84	66	175	62	2.06
1932—Philadelphia	American	44	292	25	10	.714	269	101	92	188	79	2.84
1933—Philadelphia	American	45	275	24	8	.750	280	113	98	114	83	3.21
1934—Boston	American	22	109	8	8	.500	149	84	79	43	32	6.52
1935—Boston	American	35	273	20	12	.625	269	105	82	121	65	2.70
1936—Boston	American	35	253	17	12	.586	237	90	79	130	65	2.81
1937—Boston	American	32	262	17	9	.654	269	101	88	153	83	3.02
1938—Boston	American	24	164	14	4	.778	169	65	56	99	52	3.07
1939—Boston	American	23	191	15	4	.789	180	63	54	81	58	2.54
1940—Boston	American	22	153	7	6	.538	159	73	68	62	50	4.00
1941—Boston	American	21	134	7	7	.500	155	84	65	54	42	4.37
Major League Totals		616	3940	300	141	.680	3849	1594	1339	2266	1187	3.06

Carl Hubbell

Year—Club	League	G	IP	W	L	Pct	H	R	ER	SO	BB	ERA
1923—Cushing	Oklahoma State					(No records available)						
1924—Cushing	Oklahoma State					(No records available)						
1924—Ardmore	West. Assn.	2	12	1	0	1.000	......	......	......	3	4	......
1924—Oklahoma City	Western	2	15	1	1	.500	19	10	......	3	4	
1925—Oklahoma City	Western	45	284	17	13	.567	273	172	......	102	108	......
1926—Toronto	International	31	93	7	7	.500	90	42	39	45	44	3.77
1927—Decatur	I.I.I.	23	185	14	7	.667	174	61	52	76	48	2.53
1927—Fort Worth	Texas	2	3	0	1	.000	7	......	......	0	3	......
1928—Beaumont	Texas	21	185	12	9	.571	177	69	61	116	45	2.97
1928—New York	National	20	124	10	6	.625	117	49	39	37	21	2.83
1929—New York	National	39	268	18	11	.621	273	128	110	106	67	3.69
1930—New York	National	37	242	17	12	.586	263	120	104	117	58	3.87
1931—New York	National	36	248	14	12	.538	211	88	73	155	67	2.65
1932—New York	National	40	284	18	11	.621	260	96	79	137	40	2.50
1933—New York	National	45	309	23	12	.657	256	69	57	156	47	1.66
1934—New York	National	49	313	21	12	.636	286	100	80	118	37	2.30
1935—New York	National	42	303	23	12	.657	314	125	110	150	49	3.27
1936—New York	National	42	304	26	6	.813	265	81	78	123	57	2.31
1937—New York	National	39	262	22	8	.733	261	108	93	159	55	3.19
1938—New York	National	24	179	13	10	.565	171	70	61	104	33	3.07
1939—New York	National	29	154	11	9	.550	150	60	47	62	24	2.75
1940—New York	National	31	214	11	12	.478	220	102	87	86	59	3.66
1941—New York	National	26	164	11	9	.550	169	73	65	75	53	3.57
1942—New York	National	24	157	11	8	.579	158	75	69	61	34	3.96
1943—New York	National	12	66	4	4	.500	87	36	36	31	24	4.91
Major League Totals		535	3591	253	154	.622	3461	1380	1188	1677	725	2.98

Dizzy Dean

Year—Club	League	G	IP	W	L	Pct	H	R	ER	SO	BB	ERA
1930—St. Joseph	Western	32	217	17	8	.680	204	118	89	134	77	3.69
1930—Houston	Texas	14	85	8	2	.800	62	31	27	95	49	2.86
1930—St. Louis	National	1	9	1	0	1.000	3	1	1	5	3	1.00
1931—Houston	Texas	41	304	26	10	.722	210	71	52	303	90	1.57
1932—St. Louis	National	46	286	18	15	.545	280	122	105	191	102	3.30
1933—St. Louis	National	48	293	20	18	.526	279	113	99	199	64	3.04

Year—Club	League	G	IP	W	L	Pct	H	R	ER	SO	BB	ERA
1934—St. Louis	National	50	312	30	7	.811	288	110	92	195	75	2.65
1935—St. Louis	National	50	324	28	12	.700	326	128	112	182	82	3.11
1936—St. Louis	National	51	315	24	13	.649	310	128	111	195	53	3.17
1937—St. Louis	National	27	197	13	10	.565	200	76	59	120	33	2.70
1938—Chicago	National	13	75	7	1	.875	63	20	15	22	8	1.80
1939—Chicago	National	19	96	6	4	.600	98	40	36	27	17	3.38
1940—Chicago	National	10	54	3	3	.500	68	35	31	18	20	5.17
1940—Tulsa	Texas	21	142	8	8	.500	149	69	50	51	19	3.17
1941—Chicago	National	1	1	0	0	.000	3	3	2	1	0	18.00
1947—St. Louis	American	1	4	0	0	.000	3	0	0	0	1	0.00
American League Totals		1	4	0	0	.000	3	0	0	0	1	0.00
National League Totals		316	1962	150	83	.644	1918	776	663	1155	457	3.04
Major League Totals		317	1966	150	83	.644	1921	776	663	1155	458	3.04

Bob Feller

Year—Club	League	G	IP	W	L	Pct	H	R	ER	SO	BB	ERA
1936—Cleveland	American	14	62	5	3	.625	52	29	23	76	47	3.34
1937—Cleveland	American	26	149	9	7	.563	116	68	56	150	106	3.38
1938—Cleveland	American	39	278	17	11	.607	225	136	126	240	208	4.08
1939—Cleveland	American	39	297	24	9	.727	227	105	94	246	142	2.85
1940—Cleveland	American	43	320	27	11	.711	245	102	93	261	118	2.62
1941—Cleveland	American	44	343	25	13	.658	284	129	120	260	194	3.15
1942-44—Cleveland	American					(In military service)						
1945—Cleveland	American	9	72	5	3	.625	50	21	20	59	35	2.50
1946—Cleveland	American	48	371	26	15	.634	277	101	90	348	153	2.18
1947—Cleveland	American	42	299	20	11	.645	230	97	89	196	127	2.68
1948—Cleveland	American	44	280	19	15	.559	255	123	111	164	116	3.57
1949—Cleveland	American	36	211	15	14	.517	198	104	88	108	84	3.75
1950—Cleveland	American	35	247	16	11	.593	230	105	94	119	103	3.43
1951—Cleveland	American	33	250	22	8	.733	239	105	97	111	95	3.49
1952—Cleveland	American	30	192	9	13	.409	219	124	101	81	83	4.73
1953—Cleveland	American	25	176	10	7	.588	168	78	70	60	60	3.58
1954—Cleveland	American	19	140	13	3	.813	127	53	48	59	39	3.09
1955—Cleveland	American	25	83	4	4	.500	71	43	32	25	31	3.47
1956—Cleveland	American	19	58	0	4	.000	63	34	32	18	23	4.97
Major League Totals		570	3828	266	162	.621	3271	1557	1384	2581	1764	3.25

Warren Spahn

Year—Club	League	G	IP	W	L	Pct	H	R	ER	SO	BB	ERA
1940—Bradford	Pony	12	66	5	4	.556	53	27	20	62	24	2.73
1941—Evansville	I.I.I.	28	212	19	6	.760	154	62	43	193	90	1.83
1942—Hartford	Eastern	33	248	17	12	.586	148	65	54	141	130	1.96
1942—Boston	National	4	16	0	0	.000	25	15	10	7	11	5.63
1943-45—Boston	National					(In military service)						
1946—Boston	National	24	126	8	5	.615	107	46	41	67	36	2.93
1947—Boston	National	40	290	21	10	.677	245	87	75	123	84	2.33
1948—Boston	National	36	257	15	12	.556	237	115	106	114	77	3.71
1949—Boston	National	38	302	21	14	.600	283	125	103	151	86	3.07
1950—Boston	National	41	293	21	17	.553	248	123	103	191	111	3.16
1951—Boston	National	39	311	22	14	.611	278	111	103	164	109	2.98
1952—Boston	National	40	290	14	19	.424	263	109	96	183	73	2.98
1953—Milwaukee	National	35	266	23	7	.767	211	75	62	148	70	2.10
1954—Milwaukee	National	39	283	21	12	.636	262	107	99	136	86	3.15
1955—Milwaukee	National	39	246	17	14	.548	249	99	89	110	65	3.26
1956—Milwaukee	National	39	281	20	11	.645	249	92	87	128	52	2.79
1957—Milwaukee	National	39	271	21	11	.656	241	94	81	111	78	2.69
1958—Milwaukee	National	38	290	22	11	.667	257	106	99	150	76	3.07
1959—Milwaukee	National	40	292	21	15	.583	282	106	96	143	70	2.96
1960—Milwaukee	National	40	268	21	10	.677	254	114	104	154	74	3.49
1961—Milwaukee	National	38	263	21	13	.618	236	96	88	115	64	3.01
1962—Milwaukee	National	34	269	18	14	.563	248	97	91	118	55	3.04
1963—Milwaukee	National	33	260	23	7	.767	241	85	75	102	49	2.60
1964—Milwaukee	National	38	174	6	13	.316	204	110	102	78	52	5.28
1965—N.Y.–San Fran.	National	36	198	7	16	.304	210	104	88	90	56	4.00

Year Club	League	G	IP	W	L	Pct	H	R	ER	SO	BB	ERA
1966—Mexico City Tigers	Mexican	3	10	1	1	.500	14	7	5	7	1	4.50
1967—Tulsa	P.C.	3	7	0	1	.000	8	6	5	5	5	6.43
Major League Totals		750	5246	363	245	.597	4830	2016	1798	2583	1434	3.08

Robin Roberts

Year Club	League	G	IP	W	L	Pct	H	R	ER	SO	BB	ERA
1948—Wilmington	Int. State	11	96	9	1	.900	55	25	22	121	27	2.06
1948—Philadelphia	National	20	147	7	9	.438	148	63	52	84	61	3.18
1949—Philadelphia	National	43	227	15	15	.500	229	101	93	95	75	3.69
1950—Philadelphia	National	40	304	20	11	.645	282	112	102	146	77	3.02
1951—Philadelphia	National	44	315	21	15	.583	284	115	106	127	64	3.03
1952—Philadelphia	National	39	330	28	7	.800	292	104	95	148	45	2.59
1953—Philadelphia	National	44	347	23	16	.590	324	119	106	198	61	2.75
1954—Philadelphia	National	45	337	23	15	.605	289	116	111	185	56	2.96
1955—Philadelphia	National	41	305	23	14	.622	292	137	111	160	53	3.28
1956—Philadelphia	National	43	297	19	18	.514	328	155	147	157	40	4.45
1957—Philadelphia	National	39	250	10	22	.313	246	122	113	128	43	4.07
1958—Philadelphia	National	35	270	17	14	.548	270	112	97	130	51	3.23
1959—Philadelphia	National	35	257	15	17	.469	267	137	122	137	35	4.27
1960—Philadelphia	National	35	237	12	16	.429	256	113	106	122	34	4.03
1961—Philadelphia	National	26	117	1	10	.091	154	85	76	54	23	5.85
1962—Baltimore	American	27	191	10	9	.526	176	63	59	102	41	2.78
1963—Baltimore	American	35	251	14	13	.519	230	100	93	124	40	3.33
1964—Baltimore	American	31	204	13	7	.650	203	69	66	109	52	2.91
1965—Baltimore	American	20	115	5	7	.417	110	51	43	63	20	3.37
1965—Houston	National	10	76	5	2	.714	61	22	16	34	10	1.89
1966—Houston–Chicago	National	24	112	5	8	.385	141	66	60	54	21	4.82
1967—Reading	Eastern	11	80	5	3	.625	75	25	22	65	7	2.48
American League Totals		113	761	42	36	.538	719	283	261	398	153	3.09
National League Totals		563	3928	244	209	.539	3863	1679	1513	1959	749	3.45
Major League Totals		676	4689	286	245	.539	4582	1962	1774	2357	902	3.40

Whitey Ford

Year Club	League	G	IP	W	L	Pct	H	R	ER	SO	BB	ERA
1947—Butler	Mid. Atl.	24	157	13	4	.765	151	86	67	114	58	3.84
1948—Norfolk	Piedmont	30	216	16	8	.667	182	83	62	171	113	2.58
1949—Binghamton	Eastern	26	168	16	5	.762	118	38	30	151	54	1.61
1950—Kansas City	Amer. Assoc.	12	95	6	3	.667	81	39	34	80	48	3.22
1950—New York	American	20	112	9	1	.900	87	39	35	59	52	2.81
1951-52—New York	American					(In military service)						
1953—New York	American	32	207	18	6	.750	187	77	69	110	110	3.00
1954—New York	American	34	211	16	8	.667	170	72	66	125	101	2.82
1955—New York	American	39	254	18	7	.720	188	83	74	137	113	2.62
1956—New York	American	31	226	19	6	.760	187	70	62	141	84	2.47
1957—New York	American	24	129	11	5	.688	114	46	37	84	53	2.58
1958—New York	American	30	219	14	7	.667	174	62	49	145	62	2.01
1959—New York	American	35	204	16	10	.615	194	82	69	114	89	3.04
1960—New York	American	33	193	12	9	.571	168	76	66	85	65	3.08
1961—New York	American	39	283	25	4	.862	242	108	101	209	92	3.21
1962—New York	American	38	258	17	8	.680	243	90	83	160	69	2.90
1963—New York	American	38	269	24	7	.774	240	94	82	189	56	2.74
1964—New York	American	39	245	17	6	.739	212	67	58	172	57	2.13
1965—New York	American	37	244	16	13	.552	241	97	88	162	50	3.25
1966—New York	American	22	73	2	5	.286	79	33	20	43	24	2.47
1967—New York	American	7	44	2	4	.333	40	11	8	21	9	1.64
Major League Totals		498	3171	236	106	.690	2766	1107	967	1956	1086	2.74

Sandy Koufax

Year Club	League	G	IP	W	L	Pct	H	R	ER	SO	BB	ERA
1955—Brooklyn	National	12	42	2	2	.500	33	15	14	30	28	3.00
1956—Brooklyn	National	16	59	2	4	.333	66	37	32	30	29	4.88
1957—Brooklyn	National	34	104	5	4	.556	83	49	45	122	51	3.89

			G	IP	W	L	Pct	H	R	ER	SO	BB	ERA
1958—Los Angeles	National		40	159	11	11	.500	132	89	79	131	105	4.47
1959—Los Angeles	National		35	153	8	6	.571	136	74	69	173	92	4.06
1960—Los Angeles	National		37	175	8	13	.381	133	83	76	197	100	3.91
1961—Los Angeles	National		42	256	18	13	.581	212	117	100	269	96	3.52
1962—Los Angeles	National		28	184	14	7	.667	134	61	52	216	57	2.54
1963—Los Angeles	National		40	311	25	5	.833	214	68	65	306	58	1.88
1964—Los Angeles	National		29	223	19	5	.792	154	49	43	223	53	1.74
1965—Los Angeles	National		43	336	26	8	.765	216	90	76	382	71	2.04
1966—Los Angeles	National		41	323	27	9	.750	241	74	62	317	77	1.73
Major League Totals			397	2325	165	87	.655	1754	806	713	2396	817	2.76

Bob Gibson

Year Club	League	G	IP	W	L	Pct	H	R	ER	SO	BB	ERA
1957—Omaha	Amer. Assoc.	10	42	2	1	.667	46	26	20	25	27	4.29
1957—Columbus	Sally	8	43	4	3	.571	36	26	18	24	34	3.77
1958—Omaha	Amer. Assoc.	13	87	3	4	.429	79	45	32	47	39	3.31
1958—Rochester	International	20	103	5	5	.500	88	35	28	75	54	2.45
1959—Omaha	Amer. Assoc.	24	135	9	9	.500	128	59	46	98	70	3.07
1959—St. Louis	National	13	76	3	5	.375	77	35	28	48	39	3.32
1960—St. Louis	National	27	87	3	6	.333	97	61	54	69	48	5.59
1960—Rochester	International	6	41	2	3	.400	33	15	13	36	17	2.85
1961—St. Louis	National	35	211	13	12	.520	186	91	76	166	119	3.24
1962—St. Louis	National	32	234	15	13	.536	174	84	74	208	95	2.85
1963—St. Louis	National	36	255	18	9	.667	224	110	96	204	96	3.39
1964—St. Louis	National	40	287	19	12	.613	250	106	96	245	86	3.01
1965—St. Louis	National	38	299	20	12	.625	243	110	102	270	103	3.07
1966—St. Louis	National	35	280	21	12	.636	210	90	76	225	78	2.44
1967—St. Louis	National	24	175	13	7	.650	151	62	58	147	40	2.98
1968—St. Louis	National	34	305	22	9	.710	198	49	38	268	62	1.12
1969—St. Louis	National	35	314	20	13	.606	251	84	76	269	95	2.18
1970—St. Louis	National	34	294	23	7	.767	262	111	102	274	88	3.12
1971—St. Louis	National	31	246	16	13	.552	215	96	83	185	76	3.04
1972—St. Louis	National	34	278	19	11	.633	226	83	76	208	88	2.46
1973—St. Louis	National	25	195	12	10	.545	159	71	60	142	57	2.77
1974—St. Louis	National	33	240	11	13	.458	236	111	102	129	104	3.83
1975—St. Louis	National	22	109	3	10	.231	120	66	61	60	62	5.04
Major League Totals		528	3885	251	174	.591	3279	1420	1258	3117	1336	2.91

Juan Marichal

Year Club	League	G	IP	W	L	Pct	H	R	ER	SO	BB	ERA
1958—Michigan City	Midwest	35	245	21	8	.724	200	69	51	246	50	1.87
1959—Springfield	Eastern	37	271	18	13	.581	238	85	72	208	47	2.39
1960—Tacoma	P.C.	18	139	11	5	.688	116	52	48	121	34	3.11
1960—San Francisco	National	11	81	6	2	.750	59	29	24	58	28	2.67
1961—San Francisco	National	29	185	13	10	.565	183	88	80	124	48	3.89
1962—San Francisco	National	37	263	18	11	.621	233	112	98	153	90	3.35
1963—San Francisco	National	41	321	25	8	.758	259	102	86	248	61	2.41
1964—San Francisco	National	33	269	21	8	.724	241	89	74	206	52	2.48
1965—San Francisco	National	39	295	22	13	.629	224	78	70	240	46	2.14
1966—San Francisco	National	37	307	25	6	.806	228	88	76	222	36	2.23
1967—San Francisco	National	26	202	14	10	.583	195	79	62	166	42	2.76
1968—San Francisco	National	38	326	26	9	.743	295	106	88	218	46	2.43
1969—San Francisco	National	37	300	21	11	.656	244	90	70	205	54	2.10
1970—San Francisco	National	34	243	12	10	.545	269	128	111	123	48	4.11
1971—San Francisco	National	37	279	18	11	.621	244	113	91	159	56	2.94
1972—San Francisco	National	25	165	6	16	.273	176	82	68	72	46	3.71
1973—San Francisco	National	34	207	11	15	.423	231	104	88	87	37	3.83
1974—Boston	American	11	57	5	1	.833	61	32	31	21	14	4.89
1975—Los Angeles	National	2	6	0	1	.000	11	9	9	1	5	13.50
National League Totals		460	3449	238	141	.628	3092	1297	1095	2282	695	2.86
American League Totals		11	57	5	1	.833	61	32	31	21	14	4.89
Major League Totals		471	3506	243	142	.631	3153	1329	1126	2303	709	2.89

Jim Palmer

Year	Club	League	G	IP	W	L	Pct	H	R	ER	SO	BB	ERA
1964—Aberdeen	Northern		19	129	11	3	.786	75	42	36	107	130	2.51
1965—Baltimore	American		27	92	5	4	.556	75	49	38	75	56	3.72
1966—Baltimore	American		30	208	15	10	.600	176	83	80	147	91	3.46
1967—Baltimore	American		9	49	3	1	.750	34	18	16	23	20	2.94
1967—Rochester	International		2	7	0	0	.000	12	9	9	6	5	11.57
1967—Miami	Florida St.		5	27	1	1	.500	20	6	6	16	10	2.00
1968—Miami	Florida St.		2	8	0	0	.000	4	2	0	5	9	0.00
1968—Rochester	International		2	4	0	0	.000	4	6	6	6	8	13.50
1968—Elmira	Eastern		6	25	0	2	.000	18	13	12	26	19	4.32
1969—Baltimore	American		26	181	16	4	.800	131	48	47	123	64	2.34
1970—Baltimore	American		39	305	20	10	.667	263	98	92	199	100	2.71
1971—Baltimore	American		37	282	20	9	.690	231	94	84	184	106	2.68
1972—Baltimore	American		36	274	21	10	.677	219	73	63	184	70	2.07
1973—Baltimore	American		38	296	22	9	.710	225	86	79	153	113	2.40
1974—Baltimore	American		26	179	7	12	.368	176	78	65	84	69	3.27
1975—Baltimore	American		39	323	23	11	.676	253	87	75	193	80	2.09
1976—Baltimore	American		40	315	22	13	.629	255	101	88	159	84	2.51
1977—Baltimore	American		39	319	20	11	.645	263	106	103	193	99	2.91
1978—Baltimore	American		38	296	21	12	.636	246	94	81	138	97	2.46
1979—Baltimore	American		23	156	10	6	.625	144	66	57	67	43	3.29
1980—Baltimore	American		34	224	16	10	.615	238	108	99	109	74	3.98
1981—Baltimore	American		22	127	7	8	.467	117	60	53	35	46	3.76
1982—Baltimore	American		36	227	15	5	.750	195	85	79	103	63	3.13
1983—Baltimore	American		14	76.2	5	4	.556	86	42	36	34	19	4.23
1983—Hagerstown	Carolina		2	13	2	0	1.000	13	6	5	11	2	3.46
1984—Baltimore	American		5	17.2	0	3	.000	22	19	18	4	17	9.17
Major League Totals			558	3947.1	268	152	.638	3349	1395	1253	2212	1311	2.86

Steve Carlton

Year	Club	League	G	IP	W	L	Pct	H	R	ER	SO	BB	ERA
1964—Rock Hill	W. Carolinas		11	79	10	1	.909	39	17	9	91	36	1.03
1964—Winnipeg	Northern		12	75	4	4	.500	63	40	28	79	48	3.36
1964—Tulsa	Texas		4	24	1	1	.500	16	13	7	21	18	2.63
1965—St. Louis	National		15	25	0	0	.000	27	7	7	21	8	2.52
1966—Tulsa	P. C.		19	128	9	5	.643	110	65	51	108	54	3.59
1966—St. Louis	National		9	52	3	3	.500	56	22	18	25	18	3.12
1967—St. Louis	National		30	193	14	9	.609	173	71	64	168	62	2.98
1968—St. Louis	National		34	232	13	11	.542	214	87	77	162	61	2.99
1969—St. Louis	National		31	236	17	11	.607	185	66	57	210	93	2.17
1970—St. Louis	National		34	254	10	19	.345	239	123	105	193	109	3.72
1971—St. Louis	National		37	273	20	9	.690	275	120	108	172	98	3.56
1972—Philadelphia	National		41	346	27	10	.730	257	84	76	310	87	1.98
1973—Philadelphia	National		40	293	13	20	.394	293	146	127	223	113	3.90
1974—Philadelphia	National		39	291	16	13	.552	249	118	104	240	136	3.22
1975—Philadelphia	National		37	255	15	14	.517	217	116	101	192	104	3.56
1976—Philadelphia	National		35	253	20	7	.741	224	94	88	195	72	3.13
1977—Philadelphia	National		36	283	23	10	.697	229	99	83	198	89	2.64
1978—Philadelphia	National		34	247	16	13	.552	228	91	78	161	63	2.84
1979—Philadelphia	National		35	251	18	11	.621	202	112	101	213	89	3.62
1980—Philadelphia	National		38	304	24	9	.727	243	87	79	286	90	2.34
1981—Philadelphia	National		24	190	13	4	.765	152	59	51	179	62	2.42
1982—Philadelphia	National		38	295.2	23	11	.676	253	114	102	286	86	3.10
1983—Philadelphia	National		37	283.2	15	16	.484	277	117	98	275	84	3.11
1984—Philadelphia	National		33	229	13	7	.650	214	104	91	163	79	3.58
1985—Philadelphia	National		16	92	1	8	.111	84	43	34	48	53	3.33
1986—Philadelphia–San Francisco	National		22	113	5	11	.313	138	90	74	80	61	5.89
1986—Chicago	American		10	63.1	4	3	.571	58	30	26	40	25	3.69
National League Totals—22 Years			695	4991.1	319	226	.585	4429	1970	1723	4000	1717	3.11
American League Totals—1 Year			10	63.1	4	3	.571	58	30	26	40	25	3.69
Major League Totals—22 Years			705	5054.2	323	229	.585	4487	2000	1749	4040	1742	3.11

Tom Seaver

Year Club	League	G	IP	W	L	Pct	H	R	ER	SO	BB	ERA
1966—Jacksonville	International	34	210	12	12	.500	184	87	73	188	66	3.13
1967—New York	National	35	251	16	13	.552	224	85	77	170	78	2.76
1968—New York	National	36	278	16	12	.571	224	73	68	205	48	2.20
1969—New York	National	36	273	25	7	.781	202	75	67	208	82	2.21
1970—New York	National	37	291	18	12	.600	230	103	91	283	83	2.81
1971—New York	National	36	286	20	10	.667	210	61	56	289	61	1.76
1972—New York	National	35	262	21	12	.636	215	92	85	249	77	2.92
1973—New York	National	36	290	19	10	.655	219	74	67	251	64	2.08
1974—New York	National	32	236	11	11	.500	199	89	84	201	75	3.20
1975—New York	National	36	280	22	9	.710	217	81	74	243	88	2.38
1976—New York	National	35	271	14	11	.560	211	83	78	235	77	2.59
1977—New York–Cincinnati	National	33	261	21	6	.778	199	78	75	196	66	2.59
1978—Cincinnati	National	36	260	16	14	.533	218	97	83	226	89	2.87
1979—Cincinnati	National	32	215	16	6	.727	187	85	75	131	61	3.14
1980—Cincinnati	National	26	168	10	8	.556	140	74	68	101	59	3.64
1981—Cincinnati	National	23	166	14	2	.875	120	51	47	87	66	2.55
1982—Cincinnati	National	21	111.1	5	13	.278	136	75	68	62	44	5.50
1983—New York	National	34	231	9	14	.391	201	104	91	135	86	3.55
1984—Chicago	American	34	236.2	15	11	.577	216	108	104	131	61	3.95
1985—Chicago	American	35	238.2	16	11	.593	223	103	84	134	69	3.17
1986—Chicago–Boston	American	28	176.1	7	13	.350	180	83	79	103	56	4.03
National League Totals—17 Years		559	4130.1	273	170	.616	3352	1380	1254	3272	1204	2.73
American League Totals—3 Years		97	651.2	38	35	.521	619	294	267	368	186	3.69
Major League Totals—20 Years		656	4782	311	205	.603	3971	1674	1521	3640	1390	2.86

INDEX